THE DATA BASE
ENVIRONMENT
Concepts and Applications

THE DATA BASE ENVIRONMENT
Concepts and Applications

Kenmore S. Brathwaite, Ph.D.

VNR | VAN NOSTRAND REINHOLD
——————————New York

Copyright © 1990 by Van Nostrand Reinhold
Library of Congress Catalog Card Number 90-31993
ISBN 0-442-00300-5

Printed in the United States of America

Van Nostrand Reinhold
115 Fifth Avenue
New York, New York 10003

Van Nostrand Reinhold International Company Limited
11 New Fetter Lane
London EC4P 4EE, England

Van Nostrand Reinhold
480 La Trobe Street
Melbourne, Victoria 3000, Australia

Nelson Canada
1120 Birchmount Road
Scarborough, Ontario M1K 5G4, Canada

16 15 14 13 12 11 10 9 8 7 6 5 4 3 2 1

Library of Congress Cataloging-in-Publication Data

Brathwaite, Ken S.
   The data base environment : concepts and applications / Kenmore
Brathwaite.
     p. cm.
   Includes bibliographical references.
   ISBN 0-442-00300-5
   1. Data base management. 2. Data base design. I. Title.
QA76.9.D3B692 1990
005.74—dc20   90-31993
                                                   CIP

To Monique, Marguerite, Michele, and Melanie who have all chosen different roads.

Contents

Preface

The work reported in this book was developed from notes used in courses at the University of Alberta, Alberta Government Department of Public Works, and research conducted since 1979. It is intended to be a follow-up volume to the book *Data Administration—Selected topics of Data Control,* and the forerunner of another book—*Data Administration: Future Trends.*

The main objective of this book is to provide selected readings on some topics that are currently being highlighted in data base management and control. In this volume, readers are provided with information on the traditional topics of data analysis; data base design; data base security, integrity, and privacy; and disaster recovery. In an attempt to make the volume a practical guide that can be used by data base administrators, data administrators, and system designers, many approaches have been included that can be readily implemented in the reader's data base environment.

As the title suggests, the volume provides information on some interrelated topics in data base management, but deals with them independently of each other. Thus, each chapter in the book is intended to stand alone, and any continuity between chapters is purely incidental. Therefore, the reader interested primarily in data analysis techniques would not have to read the chapter on data base design in order to understand the issues of data analysis.

Chapter 1 introduces the concepts of data administration and data base administration, showing that data base administration is but a subset of data administration and that, although different, the two functions are used interchangeably by several researchers. Chapter 2 introduces various data analysis techniques and shows how these techniques are used in the development of data base systems. Chapter

3 outlines a data base design methodology that has been developed, tested, and implemented by a major public utility.

The chapters on data base security, integrity, and privacy and protection mechanisms are a direct result of years of research and practical application in a large data base environment.

The chapter on disaster recovery is, again, the result of a study on that subject done for a large insurance company. The chapter discusses an approach for developing an implementable disaster recovery plan in large organizations.

The information in Chapters 7, 8, and 9 in Part II of the book are derived as a result of case studies done in the various topic areas covered. The chapter on management discusses several practical examples of procedures that can be easily implemented in a data base environment. Chapter 8, on concepts of data dictionaries, discusses the typical contents of a data dictionary and how the data dictionary can be used to protect data. Chapter 9 discusses the use of data dictionaries in systems design. It details the role that the dictionary plays in the systems development life cycle.

Finally, the third part of the book deals primarily with controlling the data base environment. Topics such as data security, protection mechanisms, and disaster recovery are discussed.

Acknowledgments

I am grateful for the comments and suggestions that I received from Vic Howard, Stanley Locke, Francis Chin, and Jay Louise Weldon. The initial draft of this manuscript was ably typed by Jane Cuffy and Andrea Drayton. Their efforts are appreciated. I am also grateful to Mr. Irwin Fishman, who greatly contributed to the work on Disaster Recovery.

Ken S. Brathwaite
Brooklyn, New York

PART 1

DATA BASE CONCEPTS

1

Concepts of Data Administration and Data Base Administration

This chapter introduces concepts that are pertinent to the proper understanding of the functions of data administration.

In the 1970s, a certain degree of specialization in managing the data resource emerged from the data processing function. This specialization was referred to in two ways; data administration and data base administration. Today, however, those names are used to describe two separate functions.

Data Administration (DA) is the establishment and enforcement of policies and procedures for managing the company's data as a corporate resource. It involves the collection, storage, and dissemination of data as a globally administered and standardized resource.

Data Base Administration (DBA) is a technical function that performs data base design and development, provides education on data base technology, provides support to users in operational data management related activities, and may provide technical support for data administration.

Data administration and data base administration are not the same, although several authors have used the terms interchangeably. It is preferable, however, to define data administration as that function responsible for the total management of the enterprise's data resource. Thus, Data Base Administration is a subset of Data Administration.

1.1 APPROACH TO THE COVERAGE OF TOPICS

Although the emphasis of this book is on the functions and tasks conducted by the traditional data administration department of a typical organization, the DBA functions will be highlighted in this chapter, since that function is recognized as the older of the two.

The DA functions and activities will be listed here, but the reader should refer to the literature for a more detailed coverage of Data Administration concepts.

1.2 THE FUNCTIONS OF DATA ADMINISTRATION (DA)

Gillenson defines data administration as the custodianship, management, planning, and documentation of an enterprise's data.

Minami indicates that the data administration function includes the development and coordination of the policies, procedures, and plans for the capture, correction, storage, and use of data.

It also serves to provide custody of the data and to coordinate data activities with systems developers and users.

The DA functions include:

- Logical design of data base system. This function produces a schema that shows which data fields should be grouped together to form records and files, and how they are related.
- Liaison with systems personnel during the application development process. The DA personnel will frequently communicate to systems personnel the changing requirements of the logical data base design and those of the users.
- Training all relevant personnel in data administration concepts and techniques.
- Setting and monitoring standards for logical and physical data base design, data dictionary development and content, and systems testing and acceptance.
- Design of documentation, including data dictionaries.
- Promotion and allowance for interdepartmental data sharing.
- Resolution of data sharing conflicts.
- Setting up facilities to monitor data usage and obtaining authorization for usage.

1.3 THE ACTIVITIES OF DATA ADMINISTRATION

The activities in the following list can be defined as the various tasks that must be performed by DA in order to carry out the stated functions.

These activities include:

- developing and enforcing policies governing data collection
- developing tactical and strategic plans for data use
- developing definitional requirements for data dictionary items
- developing/enforcing naming conventions

- controlling data integrity and security
- identifying potential DB applications
- planning the evolution of the enterprise data base
- identifying opportunities for data sharing
- providing data base education to the enterprise
- providing primary input to the data dictionary
- working with internal auditors in auditing the data base
- long-range planning for the enterprise's data resource
- promoting security and privacy controls

1.4 POSITIONING OF THE DATA ADMINISTRATION FUNCTION

A considerable amount of research has been conducted to determine the effect of the positioning of DA on its success and effectiveness. Some researchers have indicated that DA should be part of the traditional management information systems structure, while others are in favor of having DA placed outside of the MIS structure.

The author favors DA being placed outside of the MIS structure. DA is responsible for all of the corporation's data resources, and for planning for the effective management of that resource. This data resource should have the same status as finance, personnel, marketing, and production. Thus, for the effective management and recognition of data as a resource, the DA function should be outside of MIS and on par with the Accounting, Marketing, and Production departments.

1.5 THE REPORTING LEVEL OF THE DATA ADMINISTRATION FUNCTION

Research has shown that the Data Administration manager can report to any of several levels of management in the organization. The smallest percentage of such managers report directly to the president or chief executive officer of the organization. A larger percentage report to an officer one level below the president, that is, to a vice-president. The percentage increases as the reporting level moved further away from the president.

Kahn indicates that the form of the DA function was dependent on the reporting level of the Chief Information Officer (CIO), to whom the DA reports, with respect to the president.

It has been determined that the success of the DA function depends upon the reporting level.

Gillenson has shown that one of the inhibitors to the success of the DA function is that it is not situated high enough in the organization. Ideally, the DA function should report directly to the president, but never more than to one level below the president.

1.6 A SUMMARY OF DATA ADMINISTRATION FUNCTION AND ACTIVITIES

Recent survey and research information has shown that DA is involved in the following functions and activities:

- logical data base design (note that physical data base design is done by DBA)
- data security and privacy
- user relations and education
- policy formulation
- data dictionary design and maintenance
- conflict resolution and data sharing disputes
- promotion of auditing and monitoring of the data base
- total management of the data base environment and data resources

1.7 THE FUNCTIONS OF DATA BASE ADMINISTRATION (DBA)

Data base administration is concerned with the technical aspects of managing the data resource, rather than the administrative aspects. These technical aspects require that expertise in a particular data base management system (DBMS) and designing data base logical and physical structures be present.

The DBA functions will include:

- The physical design of data base systems.
- Assisting in the negotiation for the acquisition of hardware and software to support the data base management system (DBMS).
- Acting as a contact point for users experiencing problems with the DBMS and associated software.
- Monitoring the performance of the DBMS and the individual transactions against the data bases.
- Assisting in the development of long-term plans to ensure that adequate hardware capacity and facilities are available to meet the requirements of new systems, or expansions of existing systems.
- Ensuring that physical data base designs, and the manner in which relationships are chosen to be implemented and maintained, are such that the addition of new physical data bases are readily achievable with minimum disruption to existing systems.
- Ensuring the integrity of production data by seeing that controls to deny unauthorized access are implemented, and that adequate validation procedures are included in all transactions.
- Ensuring the security and privacy of data by seeing that controls to safeguard against threats to data bases, libraries, and log tapes are implemented.
- Providing test facilities in the form of DBMS hardware and software.

- Researching new DBMS packages, procedures, standards, and other support facilities.
- Developing documentation practices, procedures, and standards both for internal DBA use and for users who interface with the DBA and DBMS.

1.8 THE SCOPE OF DBA FUNCTIONS

The following paragraphs are intended to delineate the scope of the DBA functions, by identifying some of the main activities. These activities will include:

- The secure operation of the DBMS.
- The design of physical data bases.
- The identification and maintenance of physical data base design and usage standards, guidelines, and policies.
- The identification of hardware, software, and other facilities required to aid DBA in the performance of its duties.
- Identification of education and training requirements for the staff.
- Continual monitoring of its functions, objectives, responsibilities, and authority, so that DBA can best serve the changing needs of the corporation and its various departments

1.9 THE ACTIVITIES OF DATA BASE ADMINISTRATION

The activities of DBA are grouped according to the major phases of system development, operation, and maintenance. These phases and activities are illustrated in Figure 1.1.

1.9.1 DBA Activities During the Feasibility Phase

Activities during this phase are concerned with planning for the new application and its development. The activities include:

- Facility Capacity Planning—For each new application, a plan of additional hardware and software facilities must be developed. Also, the likely effect of the new application on the total DBMS performance must be estimated.
- Operations Staff Planning—Ensures that, for all current and future systems, the DBA function is adequately staffed.
- Development Staff Planning—DBA ensures that it has adequately trained staff to meet its short-term needs, and to provide proper support for current and projected data base system development.

PHASES / ACTIVITIES	FEASIBILITY	DEFINITION	DESIGN	IMPLEMENTATION	CONVERSION	OPERATION	MAINTENANCE	PERFORMANCE REVIEWS
	Facility Capacity Planning	Familiarization	Data Base Design	Performance Monitoring	Conversion Facility	Approval for System	Review of Data Base	Review Design Details
	Operations Staff Planning	Reviews	Simulation	Operation of DBMS Test Facility	Plan for Production System	Control of System	Changes to Environment	Review Program Logs
	Development Staff Planning		Access Guidelines			Monitoring	Changes due to Staff Performance	Integrity Failure
			Review and Approval				Revision of Plans	Security and Audit Facilities
			Test Facility					Performance Data

FIG. 1.1. Activities of DBA during various design phases.

1.9.2 DBA Activities During
the Definition Phase

The activities during the definition phase are mainly centred on the development of data definitions and logical views. The DBA activities would be as follows:

- Familiarization—a process of familiarization with the contents of the detailed definitions, the application's logical views, and the data dictionary.
- Review—DBA will, along with other teams, review the completed detailed definition documentation.

1.9.3 DBA Activities During
the Design Phase

DBA activities during the design phase are concerned with the design of physical data bases to meet the applications requirements, and the integration of common data bases used by more than one system. The activities include those listed below.

Data Base Design. The development of a physical data base design. DBA will consider several factors, such as performance requirements, data and transaction volumes, integrity, security requirements, CPU and peripheral capacity, access methods, pointers, indexing and compression alternatives, and media storage.

Simulation. Identification of the parameters that represent the characteristics of the new system, and the parameters that represent the characteristics of the existing workload. The simulation should provide a measure of likely performance, a comparison of design alternatives, and a verification of capacity estimates.

Access Guidelines. The production of DBMS data base access guidelines. The guidelines will define unit costs for access to each segment of the data base. Different costs are also defined for insert, delete, replace, and retrieve activities.

Review and Approval. The physical data base design and access guidelines will be subjected to a formal review. The review should determine whether the design reflects the requirements of the corporate view, along with any other relevant standards.

Test Facility. The provision of suitable test facilities for system development must be planned and implemented. These facilities include:

- data set space
- utility procedure
- special routines (e.g., randomizing and compression)
- hardware and software resources
- staff resources

1.9.4 DBA Activities During the Implementation Phase

The main activities during the implementation phase are the generation of the DBMS, and monitoring of the testing of the new system to identify weaknesses in the physical data base design, or a failure to adhere to standards. These activities include:

- Monitoring the performance of programs during testing. The factors examined would include:
  CPU usage
  I/O activity
  storage size
  performance variations
  program conflicts for data

- The operation of a DBMS test facility. This involves the starting, monitoring of, restart and/or recovery (when required), component backup and submission, and monitoring of batch jobs for the DBMS test system.

1.9.5 DBA Activities During the Conversion Phase

Activities during this phase are concerned with supporting the conversion process and preparation for operational running of the system. These activities include:

- Conversion facility—provide DBMS conversion facility e. g. generate the DBMS system, allocate library and data set space, and documentation.
- Plan for production system—develop plan for final operation. These plans involve monitoring arrangements, staff training and education, backup and reorganization arrangements, and correction arrangements.

1.9.6 DBA Activities During Operations

The activities during operations will include:

- approval for running the system
- control of the system and all DBMS facilities
- monitoring—continual monitoring of the overall DBMS production system's performance and availability

1.9.7 DBA Activities During the Maintenance Phase

The activities during the maintenance phase will include:

- A review of data base and program changes.

- Changes to the environment due to general hardware and software changes, DBMS changes, and tuning of the DBMS.
- Changes due to the performance of the DBA staff, and revision of internal plans and standards.

1.9.8 DBA Activities During Performance Reviews

The activities during this phase will consist primarily of providing required information for any performance review, including:

- design details
- problem logs
- integrity and security failures
- audit facilities
- performance data

1.10 SUMMARY

This chapter has served to introduce the basic concepts of Data Administration (DA) and Data Base Administration (DBA). The most important concepts dealt with the functions and activities in both areas.

The DBA activities were classified into phases, corresponding to the development life cycle of systems. Each activity of DA was listed, although not classified as above.

Finally, the coverage of the positioning and reporting level of the data administration function discussed the results of industry research in those areas.

2

Data Analysis Techniques

This chapter introduces techniques for conducting data analysis and utilizing these techniques in the development of data base systems.

Data analysis is defined as the determination of the fundamental data resources of an organization. It deals with the collection of the basic entities and the relationships between those entities.

The chapter begins with definitions for terms that are generally used in data analysis. Terms such as data, data item, entity, attribute, and relationship are defined. This chapter establishes the premise that data is a resource in much the same way as employees, products, natural resources, and finances are. It continues by discussing the components of data analysis and techniques for performing the normalization of data.

2.1 DEFINITIONS AND TERMINOLOGY

Attribute	An attribute is a *descriptive value* or property associated with an individual *entity*.
Data	The *values* taken by various data items are called data. For example; the value of the data element, Customer Name, is data.
Data analysis	The determination of the fundamental data resources of an organization. It deals with the collection of the basic entities and the relationships between those entities.

Data Item

A data item is the *smallest unit* of named data. A data item is often referred to as a field or data element.

Entity (or Entity Class or Entity Type)

An entity is a *fundamental object of interest* to an organization. An entity may be a person, place, thing, concept, or event, and may be real or abstract. It should have a unique identifier.

Entity Model

A diagrammatical representation of the relationships between entity classes. The representation allows us to include only those entities that are required to solve the user's data processing problem.

Information

Information is *data* that is *processed, accessed,* and *assimilated* or *used* in the decision making process. It is the analysis and synthesis of data.

Logical Schema (External Structure/Schema)

The mapping of the entity model into the constructs or constraints of the data base management system (DBMS). In general, the logical schema indicates how the model will be stored and accessed.

Relationship

A relationship is an *association* between two or more entities.

2.2 DATA AS A RESOURCE

Data must be seen as a resource in much the same way as employees, products, natural resources, finances, and other material products or resources.

Data as a resource must be recognized to have cost and value.

In order to exploit the data resource, it must be understood, conserved, employed, and integrated. It is necessary to learn about its nature and characteristics, how it is used, what it is used for, where it resides, and where it comes from.

2.2.1 Information Resource Management

Information Resource Management (IRM) deals with planning for, allocating, maintaining and conserving, prudently exploiting, effectively employing, and integrating the data resource.

To manage data effectively as a resource, it is necessary to obtain as much information about the data as is possible. There must be stringent procedures for collecting, maintaining, and using the resource.

2.2.2 Management Control of the Data Resource

Management control of data includes the following:

- Common procedures for access control to the data
- Establishing lines of authority and responsibility for the data
- Common procedures for collecting, updating, and maintaining the data
- Common formats and procedures for data definition
- Identifying entities that are important to the enterprise
- Evaluating, mediating, and reconciling the conflicting needs and prerogatives of functional departments
- ensuring the auditability of both the data and all transactions against the data
- Controlling the data in order to measure and evaluate the corporation and predict its reaction to changes in its environment and in its own internal organization.

2.2.3 Data Ownership Philosophies

The introduction of the data base era not only meant a change in traditional data processing, but also in traditional definitions of 'data ownership.'

In traditional data processing, total control over the creation, maintenance, and processing of data meant 'ownership' of that data.

In a data base environment, data sharing and data integration has lessened total control, and now imply a loss of 'ownership.'

In data analysis, the establishing of data 'owners' is important to:

- control access to the data
- allow data sharing
- establish relationships and interfaces between entities
- establish common definitions for data
- resolve discrepancies and conflicts over standards and conventions

2.2.4 Different Views of Data

Data about an enterprise is not singularly determined. Different people perceive and describe an enterprise differently, and hence have different starting points concerning what is to be modelled.

It's not merely a matter of scope, of including more or less in the view. People looking at the same thing see it differently.

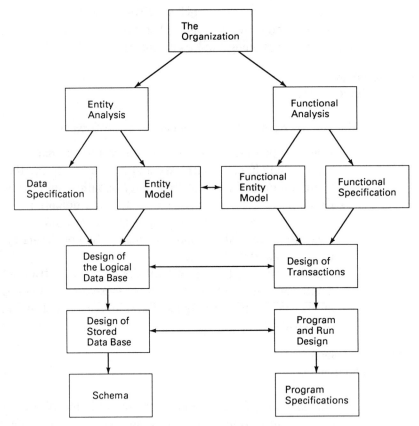

FIG. 2.1.   Analysis and design.

Examples of different views of data. The secretary of a department may be, in someone else's view, the secretary of the manager of the department.

A manufacturing operation might be performed by a certain department, or it might be viewed as performed by a person assigned to that department.

Social security number is generally considered to identify a person, but it really identifies an account that belongs to a person.

2.3 DATA ANALYSIS

The primary purpose of data analysis is to determine the fundamental nature of an organization's data resources and to organize and document all relevant facts concerning this data (see Figure 2.1).

Data analysis has been used to:

- Determine the fundamental data resources of an organization.
- Provide a disciplined approach towards cataloging the existing data, in terms of the entities and relationships represented.

- Provide an effective means of communicating with non-data processing users as it deals only with things that the users are familiar with, and not with such objects as files and records.
- Analyze the inherent structure of that data independently from the details of the applications.
- Form a basis for data control, security, and auditing systems.
- Organize all relevant facts concerning the organization's data.
- Produce a point of reference (the Entity Model see Section 2.9) against which a logical data base structure for each of the data base management systems can be designed.
- Provide a sound basis for data base design.

2.3.1 Components of Data Analysis

Data analysis is regarded as consisting of two interdependent projects:

1. *Entity analysis,* which provides a means of understanding and documenting a complex environment in terms of its entities and their attributes and relationships, and
2. *Functional analysis,* which is concerned with understanding and documenting the basic business activities of the organization (Fig. 2.1).

2.4 REQUIREMENTS ANALYSIS

Requirements Analysis involves:

- The establishment of organizational objectives.
- Derivation of specific data base requirements from those objectives, or directly from management personnel.
- Documentation of those requirements in a form that is agreeable to both management and data base designers (Fig. 2.2).

2.4.1 Techniques Used in Requirements Analysis

- Personal interviews with various levels of management and key employees involved in the processing of goods, services, and data in the organization.
- Diagramming of the flow process with which each employee is involved.
- Identification of the data elements associated with that process, and the interfaces between processes.
- Verification that both interviewer and employee agree on the flow model.

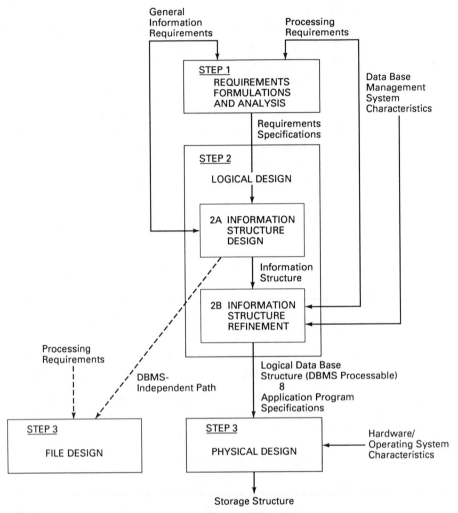

FIG. 2.2.   **Basic data base design steps.**

2.5 USER-VIEW MODELLING

User-view modelling is defined as the modelling of the usage and information structure perspectives of the real world from the point of view of different users and/or applications.

User-view modelling involves (at least) the following two components:

- Extracting from the users or from persons in charge of applications development the relevant parts of real-world information.
- Abstracting this information into a form that completely represents the user view, so that it can be subsequently used in data base design.

```
EMPLOYEE = {EMP#, NAME, SCHOOL, DEGREE}
WORKS ON = {EMP#, ASSIGNMENT#, SUPERVISOR, START DATE}
ASSIGNMENT = {ASSIGNMENT#, ASSIGNMENT NAME}
```

FIG. 2.3. Examples of user views.

There are two aspects of the user-view model that must be modelled in order to adequately represent it. These are: 1) The information structure perspective or non-process oriented view; and 2) The usage perspective or process-oriented view.

2.5.1 Representation of View

A user view is represented in terms of entities, associations, attributes in a view diagram (see Figure 2.3).

2.5.2 User View Integration

View integration is the second phase of logical data base design, where user views are merged to obtain a composite view of the organization or the requirements specified by data analysis.

User view integration involves:

- The merging of simple associations.
- The merging of identifier associations.
- The merging of entities.

2.6 ANALYSIS USING DIFFERENT MODELS

Data analysis is essentially the process of producing a mental framework that will allow the viewer to describe his view or the organization's view of data. Different people will produce different mental frameworks. There are several mental frameworks, including:

- Data-structure diagrams
- Entity–Relationship (E–R) model

2.6.1 Analysis Using Data-Structure Diagrams

Analysis using data-structure diagrams involves record types and data-structures sets, which are relationships between records types.

FIG. 2.4.   **First example of analysis using data structures.**

In Figure 2.4, there are two types of conceptual records, COMPANY and PER-SON, and a data-structure set representing the fact that each person is associated with exactly one company and that each company has a set of personnel.

Analysis may indicate that the personnel of the company were persons in their own right. This fact may be discovered at the merger of several companies, that some of the personnel held two jobs and were personnel to two of the merged companies (Fig. 2.5). Basically, the old personnel-type record has been split into two record types, PERSONNEL and PERSON.

Further analysis may indicate that the address of residence should not be in the person's record. This requires the creation of a PLACE conceptual record type and a new data-structure-set type (Fig. 2.6). It must be assumed that each person has a unique address.

It is now recognized that people move from place to place and that it is desirable to know the current address, as well as past addresses. Another reason may be: it is discovered that a person may have more than one address. In either case, a new conceptual record type, ADDRESS, is added to the structure (Fig. 2.7).

2.6.2 Analysis Using Entity-Relationship Diagrams

In the following, we shall use Entity–Relationship (E–R) diagrams to explain the previous example, in which data-structures were used.

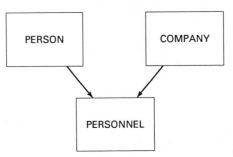

FIG. 2.5.   **Second example of analysis using data structures.**

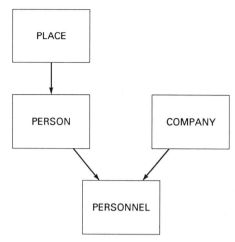

FIG. 2.6.   Third example of analysis using data structures.

The E–R diagram (Fig. 2.8) corresponds to the data-structure diagram in Figure 2.4. There are two types of entities, PERSON and COMPANY, in the user view. The data-structure set is replaced by the relationship set WORKS FOR.

Analysis shows that a new entity PLACE should be introduced into the schema. Since many persons can have the same address, a new entity is introduced called ADDRESS. The final E–R diagram is detailed in Figure 2.9.

In general, the E–R diagram is easier to use to analyze the changes in the user view than data-structure diagrams.

It should be noted that the relationship WORKS FOR can be materialized into an entity called PERSONNEL. Similarly, the relationship LIVES AT can be materialized into an entity called ADDRESS.

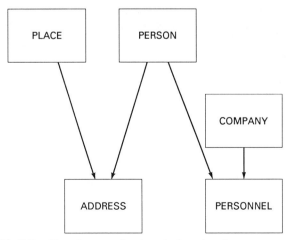

FIG. 2.7.   Fourth example of analysis using data structures.

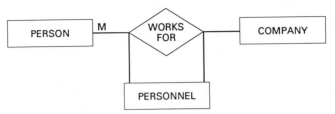

FIG. 2.8.   Initial E-R diagram.

2.7 FUNCTIONAL ANALYSIS

Functional Analysis is concerned with an understanding and documentation of the basic business activities with which the organization is concerned. Functional analysis has the following objectives:

- To determine how entities are used, so as to increase understanding of the entity model
- To provide a firm basis for transaction design
- To gather estimates of data usage for data base design

Functional analysis may reveal the attribute types of entities that had not been detected during entity analysis. Similarly, relationships between entities that had not been considered meaningful may be found to be required by certain functions.

The basic functions identified in functional analysis would be expected to be translated into transaction types in the data processing system.

Estimates of data usage will provide a means for determining which access paths should be made most efficient.

Functional analysis can be divided into the following phases:

- The preliminary phase
- The Development of a Framework
- Access Path Analysis

In functional analysis, the application area that is to be analyzed must be defined. The application area may coincide with the data area examined in data analysis, or it may cross several data areas. Here, data area may be defined as the data utilized in areas determined by the organizational structure (e.g., Accounting, Personnel, Manufacturing, Marketing, and Purchasing).

FIG. 2.9.   Final E-R diagram.

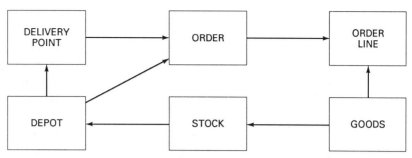

FIG. 2.10.   Functional entity model for order entry.

In the process of developing a framework, the analyst identifies events and functions. Typically, there is a hierarchy of functions, but the basic activities at the foot of the hierarchy are initiated by events recurring in the organization.

An event may be defined as a stimulus to be organization, and functions may be defined as tasks that must be carried out as a direct result of the event.

For example, and *order is placed* is an event, while *record the order* or *produce the invoice* are functions.

2.7.1 Functional Analysis
Example

One of the functions identified as being carried out in the order processing area is *order entry*. An order is received from a DELIVERY POINT. The depot that will make the delivery is selected depending on whether the goods are bulk or packaged. The order is recorded and related to the delivery point and the depot. The goods specified in each order line are validated and the stocks of the goods on hand are amended. Where stocks are insufficient to meet the quantities in one or more lines on the order, a back order is created.

The order lines are recorded and linked to the goods and to the order, or back order, as appropriate.

The functional entity model resulting from the above description is shown in Figure 2.10.

2.8 DATA ANALYSIS
DOCUMENTATION

An essential outcome of data analysis is the documentation for entity types, relationship types, attribute types, functions, and events. *This documentation is in addition to the entity model and functional entity model.* Where the volumes and complexity are low, a clerical system has been found to be adequate, but in the longer-term, and in a dynamic environment, the use of a good data dictionary is advisable.

2.8.1 Data Analysis
Documentation Examples

An example of a data dictionary that makes the distribution between the constructs of the entity model and those of the logical data base, and between the functions of the organization and the transactions that handle them, will be discussed in Chapter 8.

Examples of the types of forms that could be employed for a clerical system of documentation for data analysis are shown below. The forms are used to document an entity, an attribute, and a relationship.

For functional analysis, the access path is documented. In addition, while no information concerning attributes is included in the functional entity model, the grouping of attributes as needed by different functions are normally shown in an attribute usage matrix, where (for each entity) the attributes are matched against the functions, which retrieve, modify, store, or delete their values.

Similarly, the entity usage matrix summarizes, over all functions, the way in which a particular entity is accessed, whether by the value of a particular attribute or by means of relationships.

2.9 THE ENTITY MODEL

The major output of the data analysis phase of data base design is the entity model. The entity model is a *diagrammatical representation* of the relationships between the entities. The representation allows us to include only those entities that are required to solve the particular data processing problem.

The entity model is essentially a real-world view of the data in terms of entities, attributes, and relationships.

The model is used by the data analysis team to: reduce redundancy in the relationships; and determine which entities are significant to the model and the requirements of the problem.

Once the entity model is produced, the analysis team sets about the task of making revisions to the model.

This is done in order to:

- Produce the optimum model
- Normalize the entities
- Synthesize the relationships

2.10 ENTITY MODEL
PRODUCTION

The entity model can be produced using either a bottom-up or top-down approach. The bottom-up approach produces a composite or global view of the organization's data, based on the integration of several user views of the immediate problems requirements, and not on the inherent structure of the data. The resulting model is limited to the immediate problem and cannot reflect the entire business activities of the corporation.

The top-down approach produces a global, corporate, or organizaional view of the data first, before the applications views are identified. The entities and relationships that are of interest to the organization are identified from the business activities of the total organization, and independent of any particular application.

The bottom-up approach is the one most often used in data analysis. This approach produces a model with more clearly defined boundaries than the top-down approach. The processing requirements can be used by the data analysis team to precisely determine what entities are required and the composition of those entities. The clustering of attributes into their respective entities or the splitting of entities can be done with more precision. It is easier with this approach to determine whether an attribute is indeed an attribute of an existing entity or is itself an entity with relationships to other entities.

2.11 TRANSLATION OF A USER-VIEW TO ENTITY MODEL

A significant difficulty in defining the relationships and representing them in the entity model is in determining which relationships are directly significant and which are redundant. This can be done only with a detailed understanding of the environment, as there are no mathematical rules that can be applied, but merely patterns in the entity model, which prompt further investigation.

To determine the existence of relationships, the following procedure can be employed:

- Take each attribute type and determine which entity type it describes, whether it could describe any other entity type, and whether these entity types related.
- Take each entity type, pair it with another, and determine whether a meaningful question can be asked.
- Determine whether the relationship is relevant or not.

No less difficult is the decision concerning each element, as to whether it should be treated as an attribute type of an entity type or as a second entity type related to the first. As a guideline, it has been found that an attribute of an entity-1 is best treated, instead, as entity-2 related to entity-1 if:

- The attribute itself is found to have further relevant attributes.
- The resulting entity-2 is itself of significance to the organization.
- The attribute in fact identifies entity-2.
- Entity-2 could be related to several occurrences of entity-1.
- Entity-2 is seen to be related to entity types other than entity-1.

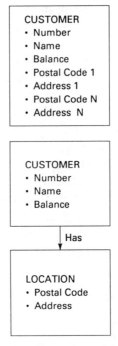

FIG. 2.11.   **Replacing attributes by entities and relationships.**

Thus, in Figure 2.11, *customer location* is seen not to be an attribute of *customer,* as a customer may have several locations, and as each location has its own attributes, such as postal code.

During the translation of the user-view model to the entity model, the most significant entity types and relationship types are defined. Inevitably, however; a model will be extended or modified during the detailed data analysis phase as a result of re-examining the attributes.

2.12 SELECTION AND IDENTIFICATION OF ENTITIES

Data analysis permits the selection and identification of entities in the following three ways:

- By one or more attributes
- By the combination of a relationship with one or more attributes
- By two or more relationships

The simplest case of entity identification is that in which each occurrence of the attribute has a unique value that is used to identify the entity. Combinations of attributes may also be used, such as when employees are identified by their name, together with the date that they joined the company.

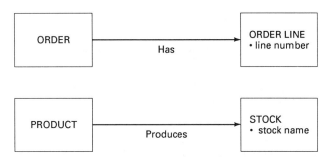

FIG. 2.12.   Entity identification by relationships.

The members of the relationship are often uniquely identified within that relationship by the values of the attribute type, but for uniqueness within the system the owner of the relationship also needs to be known. In effect, it is the relationship occurrence, as identified by its owner, which is contributing to the unique identification of its members.

Entity identification by relationships and attributes is illustrated in Figure 2.12.

2.13 ENTITY SUBTYPES

A problem arises when different functions wish to use clearly identifiable subsets of the total population of attributes of an entity type. The question then arises as to whether the entity type, as defined, is taking too global a view and is better considered as being several entity types. In general, it may be preferable to treat entities as being of different types if they have any of the following:

- Significant differences in their attributes.
- Different means of identification.
- Participation in different types of relationships.

2.14 SCHEMA DEVELOPMENT

The process of developing a data base structure from user requirements is called data base design. The data base design process consists of two phases:

- The design of a logical data base structure (schema development), which is processable by the data base management system (DBMS) and describes the user's view of the data.
- Selection of a physical structure (physical data base design), which is available within the DBMS.

There are four basic components that are necessary to achieve a data base design methodology:

- A structured design process, which consists of a series of design steps, where one alternative among many is chosen.

- Design techniques to perform the required selection and evaluation of alternatives at each step.
- Information requirements for input to the design process as a whole and to each step.
- A descriptive mechanism to represent the information input and the results at each design step.

The result of the logical design step is a data base definition or schema.

2.15 FORMULATING THE DBMS-SPECIFIC LOGICAL DATA BASE SCHEMA

Using the entity-relationship diagrams developed during the user-view modelling phase of data base design, a processing matrix that links specific applications and entities identified in the processing requirements, along with allowable DBMS characteristics and logical data base schema, can be formulated.

In the simplest case, entities become record types and attributes become item types, or entities become logical data bases.

In the more complex cases, entities can split or merge to form record types. This step begins the phase where consideration of the DBMS-specific rules and constraints must be given.

2.16 REFINING THE LOGICAL DATA BASE SCHEMA FOR PROCESSING CONSIDERATIONS

The logical data base schema can now be revised on the basis of quantitative information and performance measures.

The processing volume is defined as the combination of two parameters: 1) processing frequency; and 2) data volume.

The processing frequency is the frequency at which an individual application is required to be run.

Data volume is the number of occurrences of each record type currently stored or to be stored in the data base.

Performance measures at the logical design step are limited to: logical record access counts; total bytes transferred to satisfying an application; and total byes in the data base.

These measures attempt to predict physical database performance in terms of elapsed time and physical storage space as closely as possible.

2.17 DOCUMENTING THE DATA BASE DESIGN

Documentation is the recording of facts about objects or events of concern, in order to facilitate communication and to provide a permanent record.

In a data base environment, documentation is based on giving information about the data base itself, its contents, and its structure. The documentation focuses primarily on data-related components, such as:

- data elements
- data groups (records or segments)
- data structures
- data bases

Data base documentation covers several types of information and is intended to support the needs of several classes of users.

Seven types of documentation can be compiled for the data base environment:

- Name/Meaning—A unique identifier, it is descriptive information that conveys the full meaning of the component. The name is used for reference and retrieval purposes, while the description is valuable to managers and users.
- Physical Description—The physical characteristics of the components, such as the size of a data element or the length of a data record.
- Edit/Authorization Criteria—Criteria to be used to test the validity of instances of the component, such as the acceptable range of values for data elements or passwords for the update of a data base.
- Usage—Information as to where and by whom or by what organization a component is used, such as the programs within a system that reference a given data element.
- Logical Description—The characteristics and structure of each user view of the data base, such as logical relationships among data records.
- Procedures—Guidelines for human interaction with the data base, such as for backup, recovery, and system restart.
- Responsibility—A record of the individual or organizational unit responsible for the generation and maintenance of the data base component.

2.18 THE ROLE OF DATA DICTIONARY/DIRECTORY SYSTEMS

Data Dictionary/Directory (DD/D) systems are valuable tools for generally assisting in the collection and management of data about the data base. This data about the data base is called metadata.

The major objective of a DD/D system is to support the integration of metadata in much the same way that a DBMS supports the integration of an organization's data.

The benefits achieved are as follows:

- minimum redundancy
- consistency
- standardization

- data sharing
- monitoring of data base content
- effectively enforcing security and integrity policies

2.19 FEATURES AND FUNCTIONS
OF DD/D SYSTEMS

All data dictionary/directory systems provide the basic functions necessary to capture and maintain metadata and to generate reports from that store of metadata. Data capture implies the initial loading of the data dictionary with metadata of entry types. This capability may be provided through fixed—or free—format transactions, in either batch or on-line mode. Very often, all or part of a data dictionary entry may be generated directly from source program data descriptions.

Reporting is a primary function of any DD/D system. Basically, two types of reports are provided: 1) a list of dictionary entries, either alphabetically or by entry type; and 2) a cross-reference report.

In a cross-reference report, entries in the dictionary are associated by the relationships in which they participate. Since these relationships are bidirectional, the cross-reference may be either top-down or bottom-up. For example, one may ask to see a top-down listing of entries associated with a particular application or might ask for a trace of all entries with which a particular element is associated, a bottom-up view.

Other DD/D system features may include:

- Selectivity—Entries associated with a particular element.
- Query Languages—Available for users to formulate reports of their own choosing.
- Program Code generation.
- Directory—This indicates the physical location of data in the data base.
- Maintenance of archival definitions.

2.20 PHYSICAL DATA
BASE DESIGN

This section discusses the objectives and procedures in physical data base design.

2.20.1 Objectives of Physical
Data Base Design

The aim of physical data base design is to produce a physical data base that achieves the best performance at the least cost. The physical design process assumes that the logical design has been completed and that the logical schema presented is a true and complete representation of the real world. It also assumes that a data base following the schema will be capable of supporting the user's needs.

2.20.2 Steps in the Physical Design Process

Physical data base design can be broken down into four main steps:

- Determining and documenting data representation
- Selecting and documenting access modes
- Allocating data to devices
- Loading and reorganizing the data base

2.21 DETERMINING DATA REPRESENTATION

Starting with the logical schema produced by logical data design, the physical designer must determine how each data element, record, and file is to be represented. For each element, the data type and size must be determined. The size and expected number of occurrences must be determined for each record.

Requirements for data types and size estimates may have been determined during the initial stage of logical design.

The physical designers can provide feedback to users and system developers concerning the storage implications of their data base design.

2.22 SELECTING ACCESS METHODS

The selection of access methods depends on the organization's DBMS. In all cases, however, the way in which each record type in the data base will be accessed must be determined. Record types that will be directly accessible by their keys must be distinguished.

The access path, i.e., the sequence of records that must be retrieved to achieve a given process must be described.

2.23 ALLOCATING DATA TO DEVICES

Each record and file defined by the access method must be assigned to storage locations on physical devices. This assignment completes the physical design process. During this step, performance benefits can be gained by allocating the data base to physical devices in a way that gives priority to frequently used data or maximizes the likelihood that related data will be stored close together. This process is called clustering.

Clustering can take place at three levels:

- Records consisting of many attributes can be divided and subsets of the attribute stored together.
- Different records that are likely to be accessed simultaneously should be clustered together.
- Assign the most frequently used portions of the data base to faster, or more cost-effective storage medium.

2.24 LOADING AND REORGANIZING THE DATA BASE

In addition to developing the initial design, the physical designer is also responsible for seeing that the data base is loaded properly and for any reorganization that may be required during the life of the data base.

Reorganization of the data base may imply changes in content, structure, access methods, or device allocation. Such changes may be required as a result of the introduction of new data elements or record types, as a result of new processing requirements, or simply to rectify a degradation in storage and processing efficiency.

2.25 SUMMARY OF PHYSICAL DATA BASE DESIGN PROCESSES

The implementation of data bases from logical schemas requires the selections from the following:

- Types of logical relationships
- Access methods
- Secondary indices
- Types of pointers in relationships
- Allocation to storage devices
- Loading and reorganization of the data base

3

Data Base Design Methodology

This chapter presents an overview of data base design and development methodologies, and a detailed discussion of one of these methodologies—The Entity–Relationship (E–R) approach.

Data base design refers to the process of arranging the data fields needed by one or more applications into an organized structure. That structure must foster the required relationships among the fields while conforming to the physical constraints of the particular data base management system in use. There are really two parts to the process. There is the logical data base design, which is then followed by physical data base design.

Logical data base design is an implementation-independent exercise that is performed on the fields and relationships needed for one or more applications.

Physical data base design is an implementation-dependent exercise that takes the results of logical data base design and further refines them according to the characteristics of the particular data base management system in use.

Careful data base design is essential for a variety of reasons. These include data redundancy, application performance, data independence, data security, and ease of programming. All are important factors in the data processing environment, and all can be adversely affected by poor data base design.

3.1 A REVIEW OF EXISTING METHODOLOGIES

This section will present two of the most common data base design methodologies. In the case of the first methodology, only a brief introduction will be presented, whereas a more detailed discussion will be given for the second.

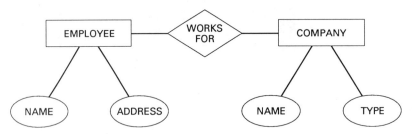

FIG. 3.1.   The E-R diagram.

The first method, data normalization and data structuring, is representative of the class of methods that take as input a list of fields and the associations among those fields. The second method, the entity-relationship method, is representative of the class of methods that take entities and relationships as input.

Data base design using the entity-relationship model begins with a list of the entity types involved and the relationships among them. The philosophy of assuming that the designer knows what the entity types are at the outset is significantly different from the philosophy behind the normalization-based approach.

The entity-relationship approach uses entity-relationship diagrams, as illustrated in Figure 3.1. The rectangular boxes represent entity types, the diamond-shaped box represents a relationship between entities, and the circular figures represent attributes.

A more detailed discussion of the entity-relationship method is given in the following sections.

3.2 DETAILED DISCUSSION OF DATA BASE DESIGN

The process of developing a data base structure from user requirements is called data base design. Most practitioners agree that there are two separate phases to the data base design process: the design of a logical data base structure that is processable by the data base management system (DBMS) and describes the users' view of data, and the selection of a physical structure, such as the indexed sequential or direct access method of the intended DBMS. Other than the logical/physical delineation, the overall structure of the design is not well defined.

Novak and Fry (1976) defined four basic components that are necessary to achieve a data base design methodology:

- A structured design process, which consists of a series of steps, where one alternative is chosen from among many.
- Design techniques for performing the enumeration required as stated previously, and evaluation criteria to select an alternative at each step.
- Information requirements for input to the design process as a whole and to each step of the design process.

- A descriptive mechanism to represent the information input and the results at each design step.

Current data base design technology shows many residual effects of its outgrowth from single-record file design methods. File design is primarily application-program dependent, since the data has been defined and structured in terms of individual applications that use them. The advent of the DBMS revised the emphasis in data and program design approaches. The concept of the integrated data base spanning multiple users was a direct result of the complex data structuring capabilities that the DBMS afforded. Data could now be viewed as a corporate resource instead of as an adjunct to a program, and consequently should have an integrated requirements orientation instead of a single-program orientation.

Achieving a design that results in an acceptable level of data base performance for all users has become a complex task. The data base designer must be ever conscious of the cost/performance trade-offs associated with multiple users of a single integrated data base. Potential savings of storage space and expanded applicability of data bases into corporate decision making should be accompanied by a critical analysis of potential degradation of service to some users. Such degradation is to be avoided if possible. Acceptable performance for all users should be the goal.

Another aspect of data base design is flexibility. Data bases that are too tightly bound to current applications may have too limited a scope for many corporate enterprises.

Rapidly changing requirements and new data elements may result in costly program maintenance, a proliferation of temporary files, and increasingly poor performance. A meaningful overall data base design process should account for both integration and flexibility.

3.2.1 Inputs to the Design Process

The major classes of inputs to, and output from the data base design process are:

- General information requirements
- Processing requirements
- DBMS specifications
- Operating system/hardware configuration
- Applications program specifications

The general information requirements represent various users' descriptions of the organization for which data are to be collected, the objectives of the data base, and the users' views of which data should be collected and stored in the data base. These requirements are considered to be process-independent because they are not tied to any specific data base management system or application. Data base design based on these requirements is considered to be advantageous for long-term data bases, which must be adaptable to changing processing requirements.

Processing requirements consists of three distinguishable components: specific data items required for each application; the data volume and expected growth; and processing frequencies, in terms of the number of times each application must be run per unit time. Each of these components is very important to a particular stage or step of the data base design process.

Performance measures and performance constraints are also imposed on the data base design. Typical constraints include upper bounds on response times to queries, recovery times from system crashes, or specific data needed to support certain security or integrity requirements.

Specific performance measures used to evaluate the final structure might include update, storage, and reorganization costs in addition to response requirements.

3.2.2 Output from the Design Process

The three major results of the data base design process are:

- Logical data base structure (user-view)
- Physical storage structure (physical design)
- Specifications for applications programs (based on data base structures and processing requirements)

As a whole, these outputs may be considered the specification for the final data base implementation.

3.2.3 The Entity-Relationship (E–R) Approach Methodology

As more and more organizations implement systems employing data base technology, the need for better methodologies to design these data bases arises. The methodology described here provides a means of mapping the entity model produced from the data analysis phase to the data base management system supported structure.

The E–R approach requires several steps to produce a structure that is acceptable by the particular DBMS. These steps are:

- Data analysis
- Producing and optimizing the entity model
- Logical schema development
- The physical data base design process

Definitions and terminologies. The following definitions and terminologies are frequently used in E–R theory and are basic to an understanding of the methodology.

A more complete description of the process is available in Chen's 1979 publication.

An *entity* is a fundamental thing of interest to an organization. An entity may be a person, place, thing, concept or event, which is real or abstract. Entity and *entity class* are used interchangeably in some of the literature, whereas some researchers define an entity as an occurrence of an entity class. For example, EMPLOYEE is an entity class, whereas S.T. LOCKE, an occurrence of the entity class EMPLOYEE, is an entity.

An *attribute* is a descriptive value or property associated with an individual entity. Attributes can be classified by one or more rules as follows, in that they may:

- describe an entity
- uniquely identify an entity
- describe relationships between entities
- be used to derive other attributes

A *relationship* is an association between two or more entities. For example, EMPLOYED BY is a relationship between an employee and his employer.

An *access group* is a physical clustering of attributes based on common usage, access requirements, and identical data security or privacy requirements.

In a data base environment using the Information Management System (IMS) data base management system, an access group could be attributes from one or more IMS segments. For example, a user may form an access group consisting of EMPLOYEE NAME and EMPLOYMENT HISTORY taken from two segments EMPLOYEE and POSITION, respectively.

The concept of access groups in an IMS environment that uses the current retrieval language (DL/1) to retrieve segments is not readily accepted. However, many organizations are using user-written routines to retrieve access groups.

Access statistics may be defined as data collected regarding the frequency of retrieval of a particular stored attribute over a given period of time. These statistics provide a means of making performance-oriented judgments when designing physical data bases.

In particular, these statistics assist in the choice of physical and logical parents, and the left-to-right ordering of segments. They are useful in the selection of secondary indices, since attributes that are updated frequently make poor target fields.

Access statistics can have a major effect on the placing of dependent segments in relation to their root, and on the decision to combine segments in preference to decreasing data independence.

3.2.4 The Data Analysis Phase

A fundamental part of the E–R methodology is the data analysis phase. This phase is concerned with identifying the data resources of an organization. Although methodologies for data analysis have stemmed from the need for a new approach to system design in a data base environment, experience has shown that the concept of data analysis has a wider applicability, whether or not data base software is involved. The approach to data analysis, the scale involved, and the emphasis placed on the various tasks that must be done, depend very much on the objectives of the project.

Davenport (1979) indicates that data analysis is used to:

- determine the fundamental data resources of an organization.
- permit the design of flexible file structures capable of supporting a number of related applications.
- aid applications development or conversion by providing a fundamental understanding of the data involved.
- form a basis for data control, security, and auditing of the resulting applications and systems.
- organize all relevant facts concerning the organization's data.
- aid in the unification of an organization by indicating the commonality between its departments and data requirements.
- provide a basis for evaluating the structuring capability of competing data base management systems.

Further uses of data analysis are to:

- identify the entities that are relevant to solving existing data processing problems.
- determine the relationships among those entities.
- establish data and process definitions in a data dictionary.
- produce the entity model.

The primary interest in data analysis tends to be in providing a sound basis for data base design. It provides a disciplined approach towards cataloging the existing data in terms of the entities and relationships that it represents. Without such an understanding of that part of the organization being analyzed, it is more difficult to establish whether and where a data base could be efficiently installed. Data analysis provides a very effective means of communicating with non-data processing users, as it deals only with things that the users are familiar with, and not with objects such as files and records.

The data analysis phase is sometimes referred to as requirements formulation and analysis, which involve the establishment of organization objectives, derivation of specific data base requirements from these objectives or directly from management personnel, and documentation of these requirements is a form that is agreeable to management and data base designers.

3.2.5 Conducting the Data Analysis Phase

Data analysis is best conducted by a team of individuals drawn from the user community, the systems development department, the data administration group, and the corporate standards department.

The data analysis team may not be involved in the requirements analysis phase of the project, if that phase is limited to personal interviews with various levels of management and key employees involved in the processing of goods, services, and data in the organization. The result of such interviews should be flow diagrams of the process (e.g., illustrations of the steps required to process an invoice, where in the organization these steps are undertaken, and with which each employee is involved; an identification of the data elements associated with each process; interfaces between processes; and a verification that both the interviewer and employee agree on the flow model semantics). Specific objectives and data base requirements should be obtained at the highest possible level in the organization.

The data analysis team first identifies the entities that are needed to solve the problems defined by the users. During the initial stages of data analysis, all of the attributes of each entity may not be known. However, as each attribute is determined, the team should document the attribute definition and role in an appropriate data dictionary.

3.2.6 The Entity Model

During the data analysis phase, the major entities and their relationships are determined. These entities and their relationships are represented by models called *entity models*. The model is a diagrammatical representation of the relationship between the entity classes.

The representation allows us to include only those entities that are required to solve particular data processing problems.

The entity model is essentially a real-world view of the organizational data in terms of the entities, attributes, and relationships.

During the entity modelling phase, the most significant entity classes and relationships are defined. Inevitably, a model will be revised, modified, or extended as a result of new knowledge about the entities being discovered. The model is used by the analysis team to:

- reduce redundancy in the relationships.
- determine which entities are significant to the model and user requirements.
- resolve nonbinary relationships between entities.

3.2.7 Approaches to Entity Modelling

There are two main approaches to entity modelling. These are: 1) the top-down approach; and 2) the bottom-up approach. The top-down approach produces a global, corporate, or organizational view of the data before the application or user views are identified. The entities and relationships that are of interest to the organization are identified from the point of view of the organization, and independent of any particular application.

The bottom-up approach produces a composite or global view of the data, based on the integration of several application views of the immediate problem's requirements. The resulting model is limited to the immediate problem and cannot reflect the entire business activity of the corporation.

The bottom-up approach is the one most often used in *entity modelling*. This approach produces a model with more clearly defined boundaries than the top-down approach. The processing requirements can be used by the analysis team to determine precisely what entities are required and the composition of those entities. The clustering of attributes into their respective entities, or the splitting of entities, can now be done with more precision. It is also easier to determine whether an attribute is indeed an attribute of an existing entity, or is itself an entity with relationships to other entities, when using this approach.

The bottom-up approach produces entity models for each data area analyzed, but these models can be merged together to produce an integrated model that will satisfy all data areas or the whole corporation. This integration phase initially involves some editing to remove inconsistencies in the type of attributes, entities, or relationships. These inconsistencies may be in the form of one name referring to different components of the model (homonyms) or different names referring to the same component (synonyms).

3.2.8 Stages of Integration of Entity Models

The stages required to integrate entity models are given in the following paragraphs:

1) The identification of any synonyms or homonyms in the different models. This task is made easier if a data dictionary is used. Components with homonyms will have to be renamed. Components with synonyms will have to be referred to by a single name.

2) Entity models for two data areas are integrated by superimposing identical or similar entity types in the different entity models. This may increase the total number of attributes in the entity type, as identical entity types in each model may have been concerned with different subsets of the total group of properties.

3) As a result of the integration, the composite entity model may contain redundant relationships. These redundant relationships may be eliminated. However, determining which relationships are directly significant and which are redundant can present difficulties that can only be solved by an understanding of the environment.

3.2.9 Entity Modelling Case Study

The following case study will serve to illustrate the use of entity modelling in data base design. The data base application modelled is a general payroll system. The

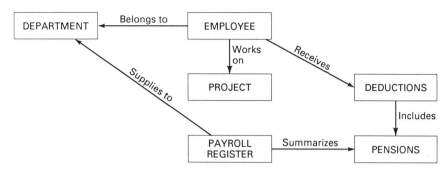

FIG. 3.2. **Entity model for paycheck processing.**

relevant department consists of a number of employees for whom paychecks must be processed. The employees' pensions can be paid in a lump sum or by installments upon retirement, death of the employee, or resignation. The department also wishes to make enquiries about projects that a particular employee has worked on.

The entities and relationships generated by the above case study are represented in the entity model (see Figure 3.2).

The model shown in Figure 3.2 will require several revisions as the data analysis phase continues and the requirements are more clearly identified. Some researchers indicate that anywhere from 4 to 20 revisions to the model may be necessary.

In the DEPARTMENT and EMPLOYEE entity classes, the attributes HEAD and SUPERVISOR best describe another entity class. We can now create a new entity class, MANAGER, for example, and replace the two attributes with pointers or relationship codes to the original entity classes. We can also add new attributes to the entity class, MANAGER.

Some typical attributes of MANAGER are as follows:

Entity	Typical Attributes
MANAGER	Manager identifier, description, authority

This revision to the model will also require that we establish two more relationships (i.e., Manager/Department and Manager/Employee relationships).

In the pensions entity class, the attribute "type" indicates that pensions can be paid upon retirement, death of the employee, resignation of the employee, in a lump sum, annually, or deferred payment.

Because of the queries users want to make, it may be decided to split the pensions entity class into one or more entities. For example, there may be one entity class for natural retirements, and another for all lump sum payments. In this case, the entities are application views of the entity class pensions. Application views will be discussed in Section 3.3.3.

In summarizing revisions to the entity model, a few rules may be listed in determining when an attribute of an entity is best treated as an entity in its own right related to the first entity. These rules are:

- determine whether the attribute itself has any other related attributes.
- determine whether the new entity is required in order to solve the data processing problem.
- determine whether the attribute in fact identifies the second entity.
- determine whether the new entity is related to the original entity.
- determine whether the new entity is related to any other entities in the model.

3.3 DERIVING ENTITY MODELS FROM TRADITIONAL OR FLAT FILES

This section discusses some approaches for deriving entity models from flat files or data bases that were not designed using E–R methodology. There are no hard and fast rules for this derivation. It would be nice to say that there is a one-to-one correspondence between the entity classes in a model and the number of files/ descriptions (FD) in a program.

However, the clustering of data items from which the logical files were constructed may not be the same clustering required for the respective entity classes. Nevertheless, the following simple rules can be followed when converting from flat files to the entity model of that application.

- List all of the file types in the relevant programs.
- List all of the logical records in the files.
- List all of the data items in the records.
- Eliminate redundancies and inconsistencies in the data items and logical records.
- List all possible combinations of entity classes from the logical records. The record name is an indicator of the entity class.
- List all codes in the records that can give the relationships of the entity model.
- Conduct a preliminary data analysis of the data items.
- Cluster the attributes into their respective entity classes.

This procedure will result in a baseline entity model that will serve as a framework for making further revisions, which will become necessary due to more detailed data analysis.

The procedure to follow for old data bases created by methods other than E–R methodology will depend largely on how the data was physically clustered for data retrieval. Very often, if the physical clustering was performance-oriented, the logical clustering into entity classes becomes a very complex, if not impossible, task.

It is my experience that the most productive method is still to obtain data definitions for all of the data items in the data bases, take the applications that use those data items, and cluster the data items into entity classes, using any known data analysis techniques.

The entity model for the particular user area can then be obtained by an integration or superimposition of the individual program-oriented models.

3.3.1 Superimposition of Entity Models

In the conversion of existing physical data bases back to their entity model equivalents, the designer may arrive at several different models, depending on the programs or applications from which the models were derived. An attempt should then be made to remove redundancies and inconsistencies by superimposing the models from several programs, to arrive at one integrated model.

The superimposition of entity models would allow the designer to determine:

- What are the common entity classes and attributes. These can be recognized on the basis of names only.
- The inconsistencies in the naming and use of attributes. These inconsistencies exist when two entities with different names are clearly shown to be one and the same entity.
- The adequacy of the model, in terms of meeting the needs of the user.
- Whether attributes clustered into an entity class are indeed members of another entity class, or new entity classes themselves.
- The existence of inconsistencies in the relationships.

The superimposed entity model can now be used as a framework for further revisions, to arrive at an integrated entity model that will serve a larger data area than several smaller applications-oriented models would.

3.3.2 Clustering of Entity Classes

Clustering of entity classes in data base design may occur in the logical or physical design stage. In the physical design stage, the clustering of the entity classes may be done solely on the basis of performance considerations.

The entity classes may be merged or split into different physical data bases, depending upon the access requirements.

The logical clustering of entity classes is dependent upon the inherent nature of the data and data structure, whereas physical clustering is not. It is a necessary, but not sufficient rule to say that attributes are clustered within an entity class because they best identify and describe that entity class, and entity classes are clustered into an entity model to satisfy a user's data processing requirement.

The logical clustering of entity classes is done to satisfy the following:

- the area served by the data or from which the data originated
- the inherent data structure

- the local view of the user
- the usage of the data
- the queries against the data
- the data processing needs of the user

The clustering of entity classes on the basis of data area is essentially done so that all data for which the accounting department has a functional responsibility will be clustered as accounting data. Similarly, all data for which the personnel department has a responsibility will be clustered as personnel data. The data areas are usually determined by the same methods as were used to create the organizational structure or boundaries.

The inherent data structure of an organization would indicate that employees are assigned to departments, or assigned to projects; customers place orders; and orders are for products. Thus, in clustering of entity classes, the cluster must reflect that inherent data structure. The inherent data structure now reflects the business practices of the organizations, and the clustering would also reflect those practices.

The clustering of entity classes on the basis of the local view of the user can be translated to mean that only those entities in which the user has some interest are assembled. The cluster may be part of a larger cluster, or an amalgamation of several clusters. Thus, if a user wanted to determine the projects that an employee worked on, the user's local views would consist of the cluster of the EMPLOYEE and PROJECT ENTITY classes.

The attributes within an entity class and the clustering of the entity classes must satisfy the queries made against them. For example, one could not satisfy a query about employees' skills and education if these attributes are not in the entity class. Similarly, a query about the percentage of an employee's time spent on a project could not be answered if there was not a clustering of employee and project entity classes.

As in entity modelling, so in clustering of entity classes, in that the object of the exercise is to satisfy the data processing needs of the user. The adequacy of the model is measured in relation to how well those needs are met. The entity classes will be clustered in accordance with those needs.

3.3.3 Applications View and Logical Schema Design

An applications view may be defined as the set of data that is required by that particular application to fulfill a specific data processing need. For example, one application may be interested in materializing employee name and social security number as its employee entity class, while another may materialize employee name, social security number, and salary as its employee entity class. In turn, these two entity classes may be just a subset of a larger set of attributes that make up a corporate or global entity class called the EMPLOYEE ENTITY class.

We may have application views of:

- an entity class
- cluster of entity classes
- cluster of entity classes and physical data bases
- cluster of physical data bases

The logical schema may be defined as the mapping of the entity model into the constructs provided by the data base management system (DBMS). For example, the mapping of the entity model into an IMS construct. In general, the logical schema indicates how the model will be stored and accessed. In the design of the logical schema, some restructuring of the model and changes to conform to the DBMS may be necessary.

The entity model is not the logical schema. The entity model is:

- a representation of the real-world view of the data.
- the building block used for further data analysis and data base design.
- not restricted to any DBMS.
- not directly implementable.
- a stable framework or frame of reference into which new entities, attributes, and relationships can fit, as more organizational data base needs evolve.

3.3.4 Logical Schema—Case Study

In this subsection, an endeavor will be made to construct a logical schema from the entity model shown in Figure 3.2. Due to space limitations, the schema for the entire model as shown will not be done. A partial logical schema for Figure 3.3 is shown below.

In the logical schema of Figure 3.3, it should be noted that the hierarchial data structure of the IMS is now applied to the entity model. It can also be seen that the pointers and unique keys are also imposed on the entity model.

If relationships other than those shown in the logical schema are required, these are shown, including all materialized attributes of relationships and their pointers. The logical schema should also show the occurrences of major groups of data or segments.

It should be noted that the logical schema for RELATIONAL and NETWORK data bases will exhibit the constructs provided by their respective DBMS.

3.3.5 Translation of the Logical Schema
into Physical Data Bases

The details of this phase depend very much on the characteristics of the DBMS chosen for the data base design.

In an IMS environment, the translation from the logical schema to physical data bases requires the following selections:

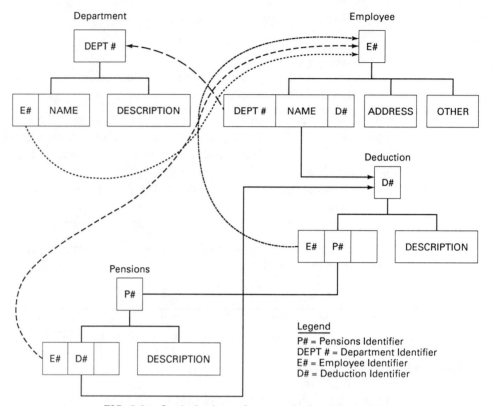

FIG. 3.3.   Logical schema for a paycheck entity model.

- Physical data bases and types of logical relationships, whether unidirectional or bidirectional physically paired.
- Access methods, whether HISAM (Hierarchical Indexed Sequential Method), HIDAM (Hierarchical Indexed Direct Method), or HDAM (Hierarchical Direct-Access Method).
- Segments and hierarchial structures and data representation, including type and size.
- Secondary indices.
- Types of pointers in relationships.

In addition to the selections mentioned above, the implementation of the physical data bases includes: 1) allocation to storage devices; and 2) loading and organization of the data bases.

The logical schema should be so developed by the logical data base designers that the only selection requirements left to be done by the physical designers would be the selection of access methods and secondary indices.

The translation of logical schemas into physical data bases is dealt with at considerable length in the current literature. (see Hubbard, 1981).

Finally, Hubbard (1981) also indicates that the following rules should be followed during the physical design process:

- Each entity class should be treated as a physical data base.
- If two entity classes share a relationship between at least one attribute and the primary key, then the structures should consist of two physical data bases with physical or virtual pairing between them.
- Parent-child relationships should be defined in a single physical data base.
- Frequently accessed segments should be kept as close to their root as possible.
- The time for searching large data groups by using secondary indexing should be reduced.
- Segments of varying sizes should not be placed in the same data set or group if frequent inserts or deletes are to be performed.

3.4 SUMMARY

This chapter has served to discuss data base design methodologies in general, and the Entity-Relationship (E–R) approach methodology in particular.

The chapter started off with a review of the existing methodologies and highlighted two methodologies. These were: 1) data normalization and data structuring; and 2) entity-relationship.

The chapter gave a step-by-step approach to design using the E–R method and cited a case-study using a payroll application.

4

Data Models and Entity-Relationship Diagrams

4.1 INTRODUCTION

This chapter discusses data models and Entity-Relationship (E–R) diagrams and the role that they play in data base design.

Data models are the basic building blocks for all data base design. They provide the underlying structure for the three dominant data structures of today's Data Base Management System (DBMS). In addition, data models are used by many large corporations in business systems planning, strategic systems planning, and corporate data modelling.

Entity-relationship diagrams, or entity models (as they are also called), are used to define a conceptual view or real-world view of data and the data requirements of an organization. E–R diagrams were popularized by Chen (1979), and have since revolutionized the world of structured design.

4.2 DEFINING SOME TERMS

Data model is defined as a logical representation of a collection of data elements and the association among these data elements.

A data model can be used to represent data usage throughout an organization, or can represent a single data base structure. A data model is to data what a logical data flow diagram is to a process (Fig. 4.1).

There are three types of data models: *conceptual, logical,* and *internal* or *physical.*

The *entity diagram* is a representation of the relationship between entity

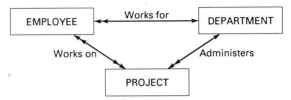

FIG. 4.1. **Example of a data model.**

classes. The representation allows us to include only those entities that are required to solve a particular data processing problem.

The entity diagram is essentially a real-world view of the organization data in terms of the entities, attributes, and relationships involved.

The entity diagram (model) is an example of a conceptual data model.

4.3 ENTITY AND ENTITY CLASSES

Entity and *entity class* are used interchangeably in some of the literature, whereas some researchers define entity as an occurrence of an entity class. For example, EMPLOYEE is an entity class, whereas P. CAREY (an occurrence of the entity class EMPLOYEE) is an entity.

4.4 SUPERENTITIES AND ENTITY SUBTYPES

An entity may be broken down into smaller subgroups on the basis of the function of each subgroup. These subgroups are often called entity subtypes. The original entity is often referred to as a superentity.

The representation of entity subtypes and superentities is shown in Figure 4.2.

4.5 TYPES OF RELATIONSHIPS

A relationship was defined earlier as an association between two or more entities. In this section, we will discuss the types of relationships and how they are represented diagrammatically.

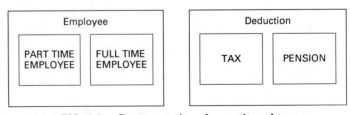

FIG. 4.2. **Representation of an entity subtype.**

4.5.1 One-to-One Relationship

At a given time, one EMPLOYEE may be assigned to one DEPARTMENT. The relationship between EMPLOYEE and DEPARTMENT is termed one-to-one. This relationship is represented diagrammatically in Figure 4.3.

4.5.2 One-to-Many Relationship

At any given time, many EMPLOYEES may be assigned to one DEPARTMENT. The relationship between EMPLOYEES and DEPARTMENT is termed one-to-many. This is represented diagrammatically in Figure 4.4.

4.5.3 Many-to-Many Relationship

At any given time, many EMPLOYEES may be assigned to many DEPARTMENTS. The relationship between EMPLOYEES and DEPARTMENTS is termed many-to-many. This is represented diagrammatically in Figure 4.5.

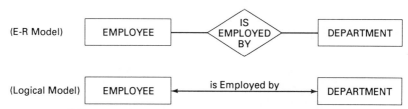

FIG. 4.3. Representation of a one-to-one relationship.

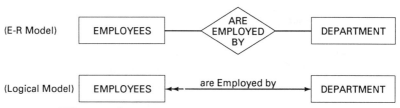

FIG. 4.4. Representation of a one-to-many relationship.

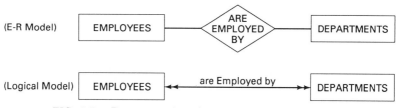

FIG. 4.5. Representation of a many-to-many relationship.

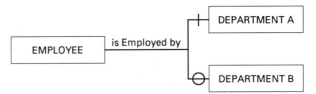

FIG. 4.6.   **Representation of a mutually exclusive relationship.**

4.5.4 Mutually Exclusive Relationship

At any given time, an EMPLOYEE may be assigned to either DEPARTMENT A or B, but not to both. The relationship between the EMPLOYEE and either DEPARTMENT is termed mutually exclusive. This is represented diagrammatically in Figure 4.6.

In Figure 4.6, the vertical bar in the direction of DEPARTMENT A indicates that DEPARTMENT A must always exist in the relationship. The circle in the direction of DEPARTMENT B indicates that DEPARTMENT B is optional. We obtain exclusivity by switching the circle and vertical bar around in the relationship.

4.5.5 Mutually Inclusive Relationship

At any given time, an EMPLOYEE may be assigned to both DEPARTMENT A and B. The relationship between the EMPLOYEE and both DEPARTMENTS is termed mutually inclusive. This is represented diagrammatically in Figure 4.7.

In Figure 4.7, the presence of vertical bars in the direction of both departments indicate that both must coexist for the relationship to be completed.

4.5.6 Mandatory Relationship

Sometimes, an employer may rule that a DEPARTMENT must exist before the EMPLOYEE is hired. The relationship between the EMPLOYEE and DEPARTMENT is termed mandatory. This is represented diagrammatically in Figure 4.8.

In Figure 4.8, the presence of a vertical bar in the direction of DEPARTMENT indicates that it must exist in the relationship.

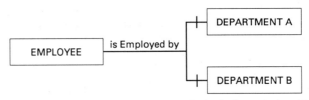

FIG. 4.7.   **Representation of a mutually inclusive relationship.**

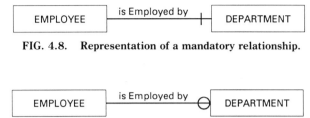

FIG. 4.8.   **Representation of a mandatory relationship.**

FIG. 4.9.   **Representation of an optional relationship.**

4.5.7 Optional Relationship

Sometimes, an EMPLOYEE may be hired but not assigned to a DEPARTMENT. The relationship between the EMPLOYEE and DEPARTMENT is termed optional. This is represented diagrammatically in Figure 4.9.

In Figure 4.9, the presence of the circle in the direction of DEPARTMENT indicates that DEPARTMENT is not required to exist in the relationship.

4.6 TRANSLATION OF E–R DIAGRAMS TO LOGICAL MODELS

E–R diagrams (models) are sometimes called *business entity models,* since they reflect the business practices of an organization, independent of any requirements for the underlying structure of a DBMS. However, in order for these diagrams to be processed by a computer, they must take on the constructs or requirements of the chosen DBMS. This section discusses the translation of E–R diagrams into Logical Data Models.

The following problem can be considered, as an example: A company is heavily project oriented. Each project has one or more employees assigned to it full time, perhaps from different departments.

Office space is assigned from time to time. Employees are assigned to an office in the department where they work. Several may share an office. Each department has one employee who is a manager.

The company needs better information on projects, project costs, the utilization of office space, and the use of employees' time.

4.6.1 Identification of Business Entities

When business entities are identified, careful consideration should be given to:

- A generally acceptable *name* for the entity.
- A complete definition that makes clear what is included and what is excluded from the members of the entity.

TABLE 4.1 Business entities—An illustrative example.

Entity Name	Abbreviation	Identifier	Description
Department	Dept	Unique ID of DEPT	An organizational unit in the company
Project	Proj	Unique ID of PROJ	A budgeted project now in progress
Employee	Emp	Unique ID of EMP	An active employee of the department. He/she may be full or part time
Office	Office	Unique ID of OFFICE	A room allocated to a department

- Identification of a *business-oriented* entity that can be agreed upon across the enterprise.

The business entities, along with their names, abbreviations, identifiers, and descriptions (for our example) are shown in Table 4.1.

4.6.2 Determination of an E–R Diagram for the Example

The determination of the E–R diagram for the example may be carried out in a variety of ways. The simplest of these is to take all of the *nouns* in the example statement and declare them to be entities and cite the significant *verbs* as relationships.

The diagram resulting from the example is shown in Figure 4.10. In Figure 4.10, the degree of the relationships between the entities may be denoted by using 1, M, single-headed or double-headed arrowheads.

4.6.3 Conversion of the E–R Diagram to a Logical Data Model

The following steps are taken to convert E–R diagrams to logical data models:

- Convert business entities to data entities.
- Represent the degree of the relationship between entities.
- Convert many-to-many relationships to associations or structural entities.
- Look for conditional relationships.

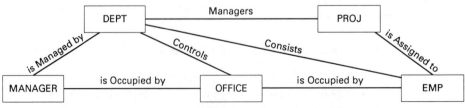

FIG. 4.10.   E-R diagram for illustrative problem.

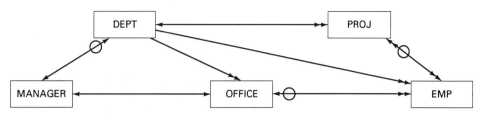

FIG. 4.11.   Logical data model for illustrative problem.

- Convert repeating groups to characteristic entities.

If we apply the above steps, we can convert the E–R diagram of Figure 4.10 to a logical data model, as depicted in Figure 4.11.

In Figure 4.11 the single-headed arrowhead in the direction of DEPT and the double-headed arrowhead the direction of PROJ indicate that one DEPT may administer many PROJs. The double-headed arrowhead in the two directions PROJ and EMP indicate that many employees may work on many projects. The circle in the direction of PROJ indicates that there is an optional relationship between PROJ and EMP. In other words, an employee does not have to be assigned to a project in order to become an employee.

4.6.4 Conversion of a Many-to-Many Relationship

Many-to-many relationships are common among business entities, but awkward to represent in a logical data model by just two entities, since completeness would require much of the same attribute data appearing in each data entity. However, there is often a need to associate two business entities, and (further) to store data about that association. Hence, for each many-to-many relationship, a new data entity is created, with the following characteristics:

- The new data entity is called an *association* data entity.
- It has a many-to-one relationship with each of the original data entities.
- It is a *child* of each of the original data entities.
- The unique identifier of the new data entity will contain the unique identifier of both original data entities.

The new data entities form an association with the two original entities, as shown in Figure 4.12.

4.6.5 Handling of Repeating Groups

A repeating group is a group of one or more attributes of a data entity that may have multiple values for a given value of the unique identifier.

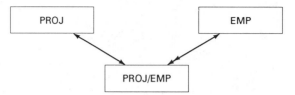

FIG. 4.12.   Representation of an association entity.

Repeating groups are undesirable because: 1) there is no way to pick a single occurrence within the group; 2) they either impose limitations or cause more complex processing of the physical structure.

In order to remove repeating groups from the logical model, the following must be done:

- The creation of a new entity called a *characteristic* data entity
- The creation of a one-to-many relationship between the original entity and the new entity.
- The use of the unique identifier of the original entity as part of the identifier of the new entity.

Figure 4.13 illustrates the handling of repeating groups found in the entity PROJ. Take an example where PROJ has the following attributes:

PROJ (Proj ID, name, address, cost, type)

where cost, address, and type have several values.

A one-to-many relationship with PROJ and a new entity PROJ-TYPE, whose attributes are: proj-type ID, type name, cost, and address can now be created. The relationship would then be as shown in Figure 4.13.

4.6.6 Translation of Data Models to Logical Schemas

Logical schemas are defined as data models with the underlying structures of particular Data Base Management Systems superimposed on them. At the present time, there are three main underlying structures for Data Base Management Systems. These are: *relational; hierarchical; and network.*

FIG. 4.13.   Representation of repeating groups.

4.7 OVERVIEW OF
DBMS STRUCTURES

The *hierarchical* and *network* structures have been used for Data Base Management Systems since the 1960s. The *relational* structure was introduced in the early 1970s.

In the relational model, the entities and their relationships are represented by two-dimensional tables. Every table represents an entity and is made up of rows and columns. Relationships between entities are represented by common columns containing identical values from a domain or range of possible values. Some of the commercially available relational Data Base Management Systems are:

Vendor	Dbms
IBM	SQL/DS, DB2
TYMSHARE	MAGMUM
CINCOM	SUPRA
RELATIONAL TECHNOLOGY	INGRES

The hierarchical model is made up of a hierarchy of entity types involving a parent entity type at the higher level and one or more dependent entity types at the lower levels. The relationship established between a parent and a child entity type is one-to-many. At the same time, for a given parent entity occurrence, there can be many occurrences of the child entity type. Some examples of the hierarchical model are:

Vendor	Dbms
IBM	IMS
SAS	SYSTEM 2000

In the network model, the concept of parent and child is expanded in that any child can be subordinate to many different parent entities or owners. In addition, an entity can function as an owner and/or member at the same time. There are several commercially available DBMSs based on the network model. Some are:

Vendor	Dbms
CULLINET	IDMS
HONEYWELL	IDS
UNIVAC	DMS 1100

4.8 THE RELATIONAL
DATA MODEL

The example discussed in earlier Sections 4.5.2 through 4.5.7 of this chapter will be used to illustrate the various relationships between the entities of an organiza-

TABLE 4.2 A Representation of Data in a Relational Model.

Department Table		
Department ID	Department Name	Department Address
101	Engineering	Building A
102	Computer Science	Building B
103	Biology	Building C
104	Medical Technology	Building D

tion. The example also serves to illustrate the various approaches to creating a relational data base.

Consider the example shown in Table 4.2. This data is represented in a two-dimensional table, which is called a relational model of the data. The data represented in the figure is called a "relation". Each column in the table is an "attribute". The values in the column are drawn from a domain or set of all possible values. The rows of the table are called "tuples".

In Table 4.2, the DEPARTMENT ID, 101, is the value of the key that uniquely identifies the first row of the table. This key is called the *primary* key.

It can now be shown how the relationship between DEPT and MANAGER in Figure 4.11 can be represented in the relational model. Let it be supposed that the MANAGER relation is shown as: (MGR.ID, TITLE, NAME), where MGR.ID is the primary key of the relation. The relationship can now be represented as shown in Table 4.3.

In Table 4.3, column MANAGER ID is called the primary key, and DEPARTMENT ID is called the *foreign key*. A column or set of columns identifying the rows of the table can also be present. This column is called a *candidate* key.

The creation of a table to represent the many-to-many relationship can be accomplished as follows:

- Create the ASSOCIATION entity as outlined earlier.
- Create the ASSOCIATION entity table in a manner similar to the MANAGER table, Table 4.3.

TABLE 4.3 A Representation of a Relationship in a Relational Model.

Manager Table			
Manager ID	Department ID	Title	Name
MG101	101	Chief Scientist	Mr. Brown
MG102	102	Systems Designer	Mr. Charles
MG103	103	Sr. Biologist	Dr. Green
MG104	104	Sr. Technologist	Mr. Cave

4.8.1 Advantages of a Relational Data Model

Simplicity. The end-user is presented with a simple data model. Requests are formulated in terms of the information content, and do not reflect any complexities due to system-oriented aspects. A relational data model is what the user sees, but it is not necessarily what will be implemented physically.

Nonprocedural requests. Because there is no positional dependency between the relations, requests do not have to reflect any preferred structure, and therefore can be nonprocedural.

Data independence. This should be one of the major objectives of any DBMS. The relational data model removes the details of storage structure and access strategy from the user interface. The model provides a relatively higher degree of data independence than do the next two models to be discussed. To be able to make use of this property of the relational data model, however, the design of the relations must be complete and accurate.

4.8.2 Disadvantages of a Relational Data Model

Although some DBMSs based on the relational data model are commercially available today, the performance of a relational DBMS has not been comparable with the performance of a DBMS based on a hierarchical data model or a network data model. As a result, the major question yet to be answered concerns performance. Can a relational data model be used for a DBMS that can provide a complete set of operational capabilities with required efficiency on a large scale? It appears that technological improvements in providing faster and more reliable hardware may answer the question positively.

4.9 THE HIERARCHICAL DATA MODEL

The *hierarchical* data model is based on a tree-like structure made up of nodes and branches. A node is a collection of data attributes describing the entity at that point. The highest node of the hierarchical tree structure is called a *root*. The nodes at succeeding lower levels are called *children*.

A hierarchical tree structure has to satisfy the following conditions:

- A hierarchical data model always starts with a "root" node.
- Every node consists of one or more attributes describing the entity at that node.
- Dependent nodes can follow the succeeding levels. The node in the preceding level becomes the *parent* node of the new *dependent* nodes.

FIG. 4.14. Representation of entities in the hierarchical data model.

- Every node occurring at level 2 has to be connected with one and only one node occurring at level 1.
- A parent node can have one child node or many children nodes as dependents.
- Every node except, of course, the root has to be accessed through its parent node.
- There can be a number of occurrences of each node at each level.

Consider the two data entities discussed earlier in the chapter, DEPT and EMP. The data model for these two entities are shown in Figure 4.14.

In Figure 4.14, Dept ID is the root note and NAME and ADDRESS are the *dependent* or *child* nodes. In the hierarchical data model, DEPT ID, and all occurrences of NAME and ADDRESS, will constitute a data base record.

4.9.1 Representation of Relationships

As in the relational data model, the representation of relationships in the hierarchical data model is accomplished by making the unique identifier of one entity in the relationship part of the unique identifier of the other entity. For the relationship between DEPT and EMP, we will have the following as shown in Figure 4.15.

4.9.2 Storage Operations with a Hierarchical Data Model

In the hierarchical data model, the insertion and deletion of nodes operates as follows:

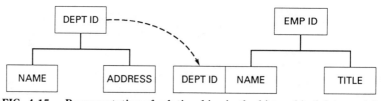

FIG. 4.15. Representation of relationships in the hierarchical data model.

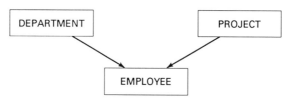

FIG. 4.16.   **Representation of the network data model.**

- Insertion—a child node occurrence cannot exist without a parent node occurrence.
- Deletion—when a parent node is deleted, the child occurrence is deleted too.

4.9.3 Advantages of a Hierarchical Data Model

- The major advantage of the hierarchical data model is the existence of proven DBMSs that use the hierarchical data model as the basic structure.
- The relative simplicity and ease of use of the hierarchical data model and the familiarity of data processing users with a hierarchy are major advantages.
- There is a reduction of data dependency.
- Performance prediction is simplified through predefined relationships.

4.9.4 Disadvantages of a Hierarchical Data Model

- The many-to-many relationship can be implemented only in a clumsy way. This often results in redundancy of stored data.
- As a result of strict hierarchical ordering, the operations of insertion and deletion become very complex.
- Deletion of parent results in the deletion of children.
- Any child node is accessible only through its parent node.

4.10 THE NETWORK DATA MODEL

The components of a data base with a network data model as the underlying structure are shown in Figure 4.16.

The network data model interconnects the entities of an enterprise into a network.

In Figure 4.16 the blocks represent the entity types. It should be noted that the entity EMPLOYEE is owned by two entities, DEPARTMENT and PROJECT. It is this fact that distinguishes the network data model from the hierarchical data model, where the dependent entity has one and only one owner.

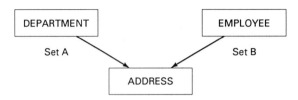

FIG. 4.17.   **Representation of sets in the network data model.**

In the network data model, a data base consists of a number of areas. An area contains records. In turn, a record may consist of fields. A set, which is a grouping of records, may reside in an area or span a number of areas.

A set type is based on the owner record type and the member record type. For example, if the entity DEPARTMENT has an attribute ADDRESS with several values, the user may want to create a new entity ADDRESS. In turn, this new entity ADDRESS may have a relationship with the entity EMPLOYEE, hence the user will have a set made up of the DEPARTMENT and ADDRESS relationship, and another set made up of the EMPLOYEE and ADDRESS relationship. These two sets are shown in Figure 4.17.

4.10.1 Advantages of the Network Data Model

A major advantage of the network data model is that there are successful Data Base Management Systems that use the network data model as the basic structure. Another advantage is that the many-to-many relationship, which occurs quite frequently in real life, can be implemented easily.

4.10.2 Disadvantages of the Network Data Model

The main disadvantage of the network data model is its complexity. Also the application programmer must be familiar with the logical structure of the data base. Finally, The programmer must also know his position in set occurrences when moving through the data base.

4.11 SUMMARY

This chapter dealt in great detail with the three major data models: *relational, hierarchical,* and *network.* It was shown how those three form the underlying structure for the three major database management systems bearing their names.

We developed some ideas about normalization, logical data base design, and physical data base design. These ideas will be further cemented in the next two chapters.

5

The Normalization Process

5.1 INTRODUCTION

During data analysis, the relevant attributes are recorded and defined for each entity type. This may lead to identification of new entity types or to the subdivisions of existing entities. It also enables the boundaries of the data area to be defined more precisely. Once the entity model is reasonably complete, explicit checks need to be made to detect redundant relationships. These checks may include the process called *normalization*.

5.2 NORMALIZATION

Normalization requires that three actions be performed on the attributes of an entity. These are as follows:

- First normal form—repeating groups are removed.
- Second normal form—attributes are removed that are dependent on only some of the identifying attributes.
- Third normal form—any attributes that are not directly dependent upon the identifying attributes are removed.

5.3 FIRST NORMAL FORM

During data analysis, *man* was identified as one of the entity types of interest to the organization, and *address* was identified as one of the attributes of *man*. During

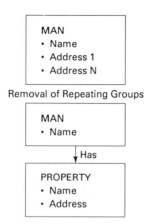

FIG. 5.1.   First normal form.

the first normalization process, it will be shown that there are hidden relationships inside the entity type, since several men may reside at the same address or a man have several addresses.

First Normal Form normalization would produce a new entity type *property*, shown in Figure 5.1.

5.4 SECOND NORMAL FORM

A normalized relation (entity) is said to be in *second normal form* if all of its non-prime attributes (attributes that do not serve in identifying the relation) are fully functionally dependent on each candidate key (attributes that uniquely identify the relation).

In Table 5.1, the nonprime attribute CUSTOMER NAME is fully dependent on the candidate key, ORDER #. That is, for each value of ORDER #, there is one and only one value of CUSTOMER NAME.

In Table 5.2, the unnormalized relation, the attribute UNIT PRICE is not fully dependent on the candidate key ORDER #/ITEM CODE.

A removal of partial dependence in the unnormalized relation CUSTOMER will produce two relations ORDER # and UNIT PRICE, which are in second normal form (Table 5.3).

TABLE 5.1. Second Normal Form Example.

CUSTOMER	ORDER #	CUSTOMER #	CUSTOMER NAME
	1	241	H. Pratt
	2	250	M. Hall
	3	241	H. Pratt

TABLE 5.2. Unnormalized Relation.

CUSTOMER	ORDER #	ITEM CODE	UNIT PRICE	QUANTITY
	1	A10	5	10
	1	C13	3	20
	2	A10	5	15
	2	B16	12	2
	3	B16	12	11

5.5 UPDATE PROBLEMS WITH UNNORMALIZED RELATIONS

The following update problems are experienced in unnormalized relations:

- Insertion—If we wish to introduce a new item in the CUSTOMER relation with a specific UNIT PRICE, we cannot do so unless a customer places an order, since we need an ORDER #.
- Deletion—If the information about a customer order is deleted, the information about the item (e.g., UNIT PRICE) is also deleted.
- Modification—Since the information about an item appears as many times as there are orders for it, modifications on the item information would be very difficult.

5.6 THIRD NORMAL FORM

A normalized relation is said to be in *third normal form* if all of its nonprime attributes are fully functionally and directly dependent on each candidate key (see Table 5.4).

In Table 5.5, we assume that a bin cannot hold stock of more than one part number (PART #). If BIN # is the candidate key, then the relation is not in third

TABLE 5.3. Second Normal Form Example Revisited.

ORDER	ORDER #	ITEM CODE	QUANTITY
	1	A10	10
	1	C13	20
	2	A10	15
	2	B16	2
	3	B16	11

PRICE	ITEM CODE	UNIT PRICE
	A10	5
	C13	3
	B16	12

TABLE 5.4. **Unnormalized Relation Example.**

STOCK	BIN #	PART #	QUANTITY	LEAD TIME	REORDER LEVEL
	210	30	5	10	5
	211	30	10	10	5
	225	50	7	7	6
	231	81	3	15	10
	232	81	12	15	10

normal form, since the nonprime attributes LEAD TIME and REORDER LEVEL are not directly dependent on BIN #.

5.7 NORMALIZATION IN THE RELATIONAL DATA MODEL

The objectives of the relational model are:

- A description of data understandable by humans.
- Query language with easily understood operations.
- To be based on solid mathematical foundations.

The objectives of normalization are: 1) a choice of representation of data with low redundancy; and 2) an elimination of anomalies.

5.7.1 Basic Concepts of the Relational Model

Values.

Integers (e.g., 245).
Strings of characters (e.g., 'J. SMITH & CO.').
Dates (e.g., 83-11-23), etc.

TABLE 5.5. **Third Normal Form Example.**

STOCK	BIN #	PART #	QUANTITY
	210	30	5
	211	30	10
	225	50	7
	231	81	3
	232	81	12

STOCK B	PART #	LEAD TIME	REORDER LEVEL
	30	10	5
	50	7	6
	81	15	10

Domains. Sets of values of the same type (e.g., all integers, all dates, all character strings not more than 30 characters long, all integers in the range 00000—99999).

Attributes. Names to which values from a certain domain can be assigned (e.g., 'EMP-NUM' could be an attribute taking on values in the domain of integers in the range 00000—99999, 'HEIGHT' could take on values in the range 0—300 cm).

Relation scheme. A relation name together with one or more attributes, all different [e.g., supplies (SUPPLIER, PART)] is a relation scheme with relation name supplies and attributes SUPPLIER and PART. Similarly, EMPLOYEE (NAME, HIRE-DATE, DIPLOMA, SALARY) has relation name EMPLOYEE, and attributes NAME (up to 30 characters), HIRE-DATE (date), DIPLOMA (a set of possible diplomas), AND SALARY (from 1 to 200000).

The domains, attributes, and relation schemes supply a framework or format for describing information. The following concept carries the actual information, like a RECORD OCCURRENCE in a file:

Tuple (formatted according to a certain relation scheme). A sequence of values, one for each attribute in a relation scheme, and taken from the domain of that attribute (e.g., the scheme SUPPLIES (SUPPLIER, PART). PART has the domain of the set of integers from 00000 to 99999).

N-Tuple. A tuple having values for N attributes.

Relation (FILE). A set of tuples according to a given relation scheme (e.g., writing the scheme as a first line):

Supplies (Supplier,	Part)
J. Smith & Co.	23456
J. Doe & Co.	23456
XYZ Co.	12987
Honest Ed's	76543

Relation instance. The same thing as a relation, but emphasizes that the relation scheme or even just the relation name is not meant.

Constraint. A restriction placed on allowable values for an Attribute or on allowable tuples in a relation Scheme (e.g., SALARY LT $150000 is a constraint on the value of attribute salary). In EMPLOYEE (NAME, HIRE-DATE, DIPLOMA, SALARY) we only allow tuples such that two tuples with the same HIRE-DATE and DIPLOMA have the same SALARY value (the *functional dependency* constraint).

Database scheme. A set of relation schemes, such as:
EMPLOYEE (NAME, HIRE-DATE, DIPLOMA, SALARY)
INVENTORY (PART, QUANTITY, LOCATION)
SUPPLIES (SUPPLIER, PART).

Data base. A set of relations, one for each relation scheme, in a data base scheme. For example:

Employee	Name,	Hire-Date,	Diploma,	Salary
	J. HENRY	AUG 1,82	LIBRARIAN	18000
	P. JONES	APR. 15,82	H. S. LEAVING	12000
	C. CLARK	JUL. 1,54	ELECTRICIAN	45000

Inventory	Part,	Quantity,	Location
	23456	15	EDMONTON
	23457	23	CALGARY
	14345	1	RED DEER

Supplies	Supplier,	Part
	J. SMITH & CO.	23456
	J. DOE & CO.	76543

5.7.2 The First Normal Form (1NF)-Revisited

Attributes take on simple values, not values with component parts (e.g., HEIGHT takes on integer values, PART takes on part numbers in the range 00000 to 99999 as values). Sets are also not allowed as values in 1NF: the attribute CHILDREN could have as a value {John, David, Casey}, but not in a 1NF relation.

A questionable case: Date has a value of the form YEAR.MONTH.DAY (e.g., 83-11-26). Date can be an attribute of a 1NF relation. However, the component parts of a date cannot be extracted separately by relational data base query languages. An alternative is to use three attributes: YEAR, MONTH, DAY.

Putting a relation into 1NF (example):

Supplies	Supplier,	Part
	J. SMITH & CO.	{12345, 76543, 23145}
	J. DOE & CO.	{34345, 98987}

becomes:

Supplies	Supplier,	Part
	J. SMITH & CO.	12345
	J. SMITH & CO.	76543
	J. SMITH & CO.	23145
	J. DOE & CO.	34345
	J. DOE & CO.	98987

Advantages of 1NF.

- Queries based on any values, using the relational operators provided in relational systems can be answered.
- The size of storage for a tuple can be fixed.

Disadvantages of 1NF.

- Repetitions of values are apparent (e.g., the supplier name is repeated for each part above).
- We may find it easier to think of values as an aggregate or set (e.g., children).

Implementation. There is no reason why relations have to be stored in 1NF form. That form is mainly useful for users of the system, so that they can understand the data in the data base system and can formulate queries that are independent of the storage format.

Physical data independence. The way in which data is stored can be changed without any changes to the conceptual model of the data or to the applications programs.

Logical data independence. Even the conceptual model of the data can be changed, due to growth or restructuring, without having to change the applications programs or compromise user familiarity.

5.7.3 Functional Dependency (FD)

This is a property of data (i.e., tuples) in a relation whereby, given the value for each one of a set of attributes $A1,...An$, no matter how many tuples contain that combination of values, the values of the attributes $B1,..., Bm$ are always the same in all of those tuples.

Example.

Employee	Name,	Hire-Date,	Diploma,	Salary
	J. S.	NOV. 1,76	B.SC.	20000
	J. D.	MAY 1,77	PH.D.	40000
	H. S.	NOV. 1,76	B.SC.	20000
	A. A.	MAY 1,77	M.SC.	30000
	M. B.	MAR. 1,80	M.SC.	20000
	Q. K.	NOV. 1,76	B.SC.	20000
	N. N.	MAY. 1,77	PH.D.	40000

A1 = HIRE-DATE and A2 = DIPLOMA together determine B1 = SALARY.

Notation for FDs.

$$A1,...,An \rightarrow B1,...,Bm$$

(e.g., [HIRE-DATE, DIPLOMA → SALARY], spoken as: "Hire-date, Diploma determine Salary").

In the above example, adding one tuple

H. D. NOV. 1, 76 B.SC. 22000

would completely destroy the FD. An FD that holds all of the time is called an FD constraint. other FDs may hold only some of the time (e.g., MANAGER → DEPARTMENT holds only until a manager has to take on more than one department; EMPLOYEE → SPOUSE holds only in countries where monogamy is practiced).

More examples of FDs. With one attribute on the left, and one on the right, the relation

MANAGES (DEPARTMENT, MANAGER)

yields DEPARTMENT → MANAGER.

With one attribute on the left with several on the right, the relation

(ADMIN-UNIT, SUB-UNIT, MGR-SUB-UNIT)

yields SUB-UNIT → ADMIN-UNIT, MGR-SUB-UNIT.

Several attributes on the left, with one on the right, yields HIRE-DATE, DIPLOMA → SALARY.

Special case of an FD: The candidate key (or superkey). Suppose the left side and the right side of an FD contain (between them) all of the attributes in the relation scheme. Then, given values for the attributes on the left, there is (at most) one tuple in the relation which can have those values. The attributes on the left form what is called a superkey or candidate key.

Example: in EMPLOYEE (NAME, HIRE-DATE, DIPLOMA, SALARY, BENEFITS),

NAME, HIRE-DATE, DIPLOMA → SALARY, BENEFITS

so NAME, HIRE-DATE, DIPLOMA form a superkey.

An example with several attributes on the left and several on the right, such as

EMPLOYEE (NAME, HIRE-DATE, DIPLOMA, SALARY, BENEFITS)

produces HIRE-DATE, DIPLOMA → SALARY, BENEFITS.

General situation in designing a data base. Think of every relation scheme as having associated with it a family of FD constraints (as well as, perhaps, other constraints). The properties of the data embodied in these constraints are used to replace the original relations with other relations that are more appropriate.

Keys. These are minimal superkeys: If an FD whose left side is a superkey cannot have any attributes removed from it without destroying the property such that the remaining set of attributes on the left determines, all other attributes in the relation, then the left side of the FD is called a key.

For example:

In EMPLOYEE (NAME, HIRE-DATE, DIPLOMA, SALARY, BENEFITS):

$$NAME \rightarrow HIRE\text{-}DATE, DIPLOMA, SALARY, BENEFITS$$

so NAME is a key (as well as being a superkey).

However, NAME, HIRE-DATE, DIPLOMA is a superkey but not a key, since the set is not a minimal superkey.

5.8 PARTIAL DEPENDENCY

This represents a nontrivial functional dependency of an attribute or attributes on some, but not all, of a set of attributes forming a key.

For example, consider the relation:

Supplies	Supplier	Address	Item	Price
	S1	A1	I1	P1
	S1	A1	I2	P2
	S1	A1	I3	P3
	S2	A2	I1	P4
	S2	A2	I2	P5

Here: SUPPLIER → ADDRESS
SUPPLIER, ITEM → PRICE
Key: SUPPLIER, ITEM

SUPPLIER alone is not a key, hence
SUPPLIER → ADDRESS is a partial dependency.

5.8.1 Second Normal Form (2NF)-Revisited

A relation is in 2NF if it is in 1NF and there are no partial dependencies.

To move into 2NF the attributes on the right of a partial dependency are taken out of the relation and put into another one, along with the other attributes of the partial dependency.

For example, in the previous example, ADDRESS is taken out of the original relation, leaving:

SUPPLIES (SUPPLIER, ITEM, PRICE)

and a second relation is created

LOCATION (SUPPLIER ADDRESS)

this eliminates the partial dependency of ADDRESS on SUPPLIER.

5.8.2 Another Harmful FD-Type

In the relation scheme

EMPLOYEE (NAME, HIRE-DATE, DIPLOMA, SALARY)

there is an FD: HIRE-DATE, DIPLOMA → SALARY. However, HIRE-DATE and DIPLOMA together do not form a superkey (NAME is a key), so there may be several tuples with the same HIRE-DATE, DIPLOMA, and consequently the same SALARY information.

5.8.3 Transitive Dependencies

The redundancy in the above example is due to what is called a transitive dependency: a set of attributes that is not a superkey forms the left side of a nontrivial FD; the right-hand side is an attribute that is not part of any key (a "nonprime" attribute).

5.9 THE RELATIONAL DATA MODEL (3NF)

Transitive dependencies can still occur even for 2NF relations, so (in order to eliminate them) CODD introduced *third normal form* (3NF). The relation (3NF) is in 2NF and there are no transitive dependencies.

Putting Bernstein's Algorithm into 3NF:

- Input: A relation scheme plus a collection of FDs for it.

- Output: Several relation schemes in 3NF, equivalent to the original scheme.

5.10 BOYCE-CODD NORMAL FORM (BCNF)

A relation is in BCNF if, for any nontrivial FD holding in it, say A1, A2,. . .,An → B, with B not one of the A's, the left side is a superkey of the relation.

note that:

- A partial dependency violates BCNF, since its left side isn't a superkey.
- A transitive dependency violates BCNF, since its left side isn't a superkey.
- Hence BCNF is a stronger condition to impose than 2NF or 3NF.

5.10.1 Redundancy Reduction Due to BCNF

In any relation in BCNF, an FD A1, A2,. . .,An → B never gives rise to more than one tuple having specific A1, A2,. . .,An values, since the left side is a superkey.

5.10.2 Decomposing a Relation into a Collection of BCNF Relations

1. Find an FD $A1,\ldots,An \rightarrow B1,\ldots,Bm$ whose left side is not a superkey and whose right side is *as large as possible*.
2. Replace the original relation with two relations, the first one obtained by removing $B1,\ldots,Bm$ from the original relation, and the second one having only $A1,\ldots,An,\ B1,\ldots,Bm$ as attributes.
3. Keep doing this until all relations are BCNF.

5.10.3 Natural Joins

Sometimes a relation has a meaning that involves "and"-ing two statements (e.g., supplier X has address Y and supplies item Z. In this case, obvious redundancy arises if the relation is stored as a flat file:

Address & Supplies	Supplier,	Address,	Item
	J. SMITH & CO.	EDMONTON	12345
	J. SMITH & CO.	CALGARY	76543
	J. SMITH & CO.	RED DEER	45634
	J. SMITH & CO. . . .	EDMONTON	76543

Get all combinations of EDMONTON, CALGARY, RED DEER with 12345, 76543, 45634; then go on to J. DOE & CO.

5.10.4 A Better Way to Represent the Information

Break the relation up into two relations:

Location	(Supplier,	Address)
	J. SMITH & CO.	EDMONTON
	J. SMITH & CO.	CALGARY
	J. SMITH & CO.	RED DEER
	J. DOE & CO.	ETC.

Supplies	(Supplier,	Item)
	J. SMITH & CO.	12345
	J. SMITH & CO.	76543
	J. SMITH & CO.	45634
	J. DOE & CO.	ETC.

Savings. There are six tuples for J. SMITH & CO. here, but there were nine before. If J. SMITH & CO. has 3 locations and manufactures 100 items, there would be 300 tuples for J. SMITH & CO. in the relation with the three attributes, but only 103 tuples if we decompose it into two relations!

5.11 FOURTH NORMAL FORM (4NF)

A relation is in 4NF if it is in BCNF and if it is not a natural join, as cited earlier.

The existence of a natural join is sometimes referred to as a multivalued dependency (MVD).

[E.G., above SUPPLIER $\rightarrow\rightarrow$ ADDRESS and SUPPLIER $\rightarrow\rightarrow$ ITEM (SUPPLIER multi-determines ITEM, etc.)]

5.11.1 Putting a Relation into 4NF

Whenever an MVD is detected, decompose the relation into two. Whenever a nontrivial FD is detected, decompose it if the left side is not a superkey (there are some details of this which are skipped over).

5.12 NETWORK— RELATIONAL COMPARISON

In a network data base, the links between the owner records and the member records in a set allow the information in the owner records to be available when processing the members [e.g., OWNER = SUPPLIER, ADDRESS; MEMBERS = PARTS. J. SMITH & CO., EDMONTON can have, as owner, members 12345, 76543, 45634].

In the relational approach, there are no information-bearing links! to link the parts to their owner in a relational model, we need to include a key for the owner record in the member record, for instance:

J. SMITH & CO. 12345
J. SMITH & CO. 76543
J. SMITH & CO. 45634

5.12.1 Using Relational Design Methods for Network Data Bases

If we have a relational model and we want to express it as a network, we can find the FDs and MVDs and use them to design a network structure, modifying it as required for efficiency.

5.12.2 Multiple Data Model
Implementations

The relational model can actually be implemented on top of a network data base.

There have been attempts to create multiple data model data bases, so that some users can access data relationally and others via a network.

This is a very active area of current research.

5.13 SUMMARY

This chapter dealt with the normalization process in a mathematically vigorous manner. The intent here was to appeal to those readers who treat normalization in a very theoretical way.

For those whose mathematics is somewhat suspect, I have devoted the first few sections of this chapter.

6

Logical and Physical Data Base Design

6.1 INTRODUCTION

This chapter discusses the two major phases of data base development. In the first phase, logical data base design, the author will take the user requirements, as represented by a data model, superimpose the constructs of the DBMS, and obtain input to the second phase, the physical data base design. In the second phase, the primary concern is storing the data, as defined in the logical data model, and defining access paths to the stored data.

6.2 THE SYSTEMS DEVELOPMENT LIFE CYCLE

In Chapter 1, two development life cycles for the development of data bases were discussed. In both cycles, a lot of emphasis was placed on the processes and functions that were required to satisfy the user requirements. The emphasis will now move away (somewhat) from that approach and adopt an approach where the data is the driving force behind the data base development activities. The phases of this approach are shown in Table 6.1.

6.2.1 The User Requirements Phase

The User Requirements phase has been discussed at some length in Chapter 2. However, in this section, there will be a concentration on those areas that are more data related.

TABLE 6.1. **The phases of a Data-driven SDLC.**

Traditional	Data-Driven
1. Identification Phase	1. User Requirements
Initiation	Initial survey
Initial survey	Data definitions
	Feasibility study
	Project scope
	Security plans
2. Systems Study Phase	2. Logical Design
Feasibility study	Data model
General systems study	Dictionary population
	Process definitions
	Program specifications
	Systems test plans
	Normalization
3. Systems Development Phase	3. Physical Design
Detail systems design	Program development
Data conversion plan	Physical data base design
Program specification	Database loading
System test plan	Testing
Manual practices	Training
4. Systems Implementation	4. Evaluation
Program development	Monitoring
Data conversion	Performance tuning
Systems testing	Reorganization
Training	Auditing
Parallel operations	
5. Evaluation	

During the *Initial Survey* subphase, the analyst seeks to determine the entities and relationships that are of interest to the users.

In the *Data Definition* subphase, the analyst obtains descriptions, functions, data characteristics, and editing rules about the entities and all known attributes.

In the *Project Scope* subphase, the analyst obtains metadata about the boundaries of the data model, the common usage of items in the user views, and information on what should not be included in the project.

In the *Security Plans* subphase, the analyst obtains information on the security, privacy, and integrity requirements of the data that will be processed by the system. He begins to formulate plans and policies for the protection of that data.

6.2.2 The Logical Design Phase

In the *Data Model* subphase of logical data base design, the analyst creates a data model of the entities and relationships that were described to him in the User Requirements phase. The model is superimposed with the constructs of the relevant DBMS. It is during this phase that some attention is paid to key selection and access methods.

In the *Usage Statistics* subphase, the analyst collects information about the volume of data to be processed, the processing frequencies, the variations in volumes, the volatility of the data, and plans for access to the data other than by unique keys.

In the *Normalization* subphase, the analyst seeks to ensure that all attributes clearly belong to the entities they best describe. He ensures that existing entities cannot be further collapsed into other entities and that attributes cannot be further grouped into other entities.

In the *Data Dictionary Population* subphase, the analyst begins to enter all of the collected metadata about the entities, attributes, relationships, data models, and the processes into the corporate data dictionary. This process is usually started in the Data Definition subphase but must be emphasized in this subphase.

6.2.3 The Physical Design Phase

In the Physical Design phase, the analyst takes the data model from the Logical Design phase as input, selects the best storage and accessing methods, and produces the physical data model.

It is during this phase that storage and time estimates for the chosen DBMS are calculated.

The analyst may split existing entities in the logical data model or collapse entities in order to improve performance, reduce redundancy in storage, or to adhere to access methods requirements. The resulting physical model may differ greatly from the input logical model.

In the *Data Base Loading* subphase, the analyst uses a data base specific utility to load data into storage areas on the relevant storage devices.

6.2.4 The Evaluation Phase

During the Evaluation phase, the performance of the DBMS is monitored to determine whether it meets the user's expectations for response time and throughput. The data base is stress-tested for large volumes of data. The pointers and chains are tested to prove their ability to return data items from the lowest levels of the hierarchy.

In the *Performance Tuning* step, utilities are run against the data base to repair broken pointers and chains. Transaction rates, mixes, and processing regions are examined to ensure that the system is performing adequately. The analyst must re-examine the main storage space, DASD space, channels, and teleprocessing lines to ensure that the data base is doing the work required of it.

In the *Reorganization* phase, the analyst reorganizes or restructures the data base in order to recapture all unused space between the valid records as a result of the deletion of some records. He also reorganizes the data base to prevent fragmentation of space, the creation of long chains, and excessive fetch times. The analyst may also want to rearrange the records so that, for most of them, they physical sequence is the same as their logical sequence. There may also be a desire to reorganize the data base so that the frequently accessed records may be stored on a high-speed medium, whereas the rarely accessed records are stored on a slower-speed medium.

In the case of a sequentially organized data base, reorganization may take the form of combining the old data base records with the transaction log file to form a new data base. In an indexed sequentially organized data base, reorganization means taking all of the data base records from the prime and overflow areas and reloading the data base without any records going into the overflow area.

In the *Auditing* phase, the internal auditors examine the audit trails, the transaction log file, the backup and recovery procedures, and all relevant standards and procedures that have been developed during the data base development period, to determine their adequacy and their ability to ensure the security, privacy, and integrity of the stored data.

6.2.5 Data-Related Activities During the SDLC

In a data-driven systems development life cycle, the analyst, data administrator, data base administrator, and system designer carry out activities and produce output, some of which are distinctly data related. These activities and output differ greatly from those that are strictly process-driven or process related. I have summarized these activities and output in Table 6.2.

6.3 LOGICAL DESIGN OF DATA BASES

The logical design of data bases is mainly concerned with superimposing the constructs of the DBMS on the logical data model. As mentioned earlier, these constructs fall into three categories: hierarchical, relational, and network.

In this section of the chapter, we will develop various logical models of a data base, using each of the three structures.

6.3.1 Mapping to a Hierarchical Data Model

The steps to follow in deriving a logical hierarchical data base from the logical data model are as follows:

- Derive a hierarchical data model including the constructs of the DBMS.
- Refine the data model according to performance requirements.

TABLE 6.2. Data-related Activities and Deliverables.

Traditional	Data Activities	Data Output

1. Identification
   Initiation
   Initial Survey
	1. User requirement
	   Define the entities that
	   will be included in the
	   project scope
		Data dictionary
		containing data
		items, valida-
		tion rules, and
		other defini-
		tions.

2. Systems study
   Feasibility study
   Data conversion plan
   Program specifications
   Systems test plan
   Manual practices
	2. Logical design
	   Identify relationships
	   among data items
	   Normalize user views
	   Produce a logical data
	   model
		Logical data
		base and data
		model

3. Systems development
   Detail systems design
 	
   Data conversion
   Plan
   Program specification
   Systems test plan
   Manual practices
	3. Physical design
	   Develop a physical data
	   base from the logical
	   model
	   Verify adequacy of
	   physical design
		Data dictionary
		with all physi-
		data flows

4. Systems Implementation
   Program development
 	
   Data conversion
 	
   Systems testing
   Training
   Parallel operations
5. Evaluation
	4. Evaluation
	   Assist DBA in setting
	   procedures for monitoring
	   the data base
	   Assist auditors in setting
	   procedures for auditing
	   the data base	

- Select key names.
- Add relationships, association, and characteristic entities as required by the particular DBMS.

In deriving a hierarchical data model that includes the constructs of the DBMS, it may be desirous to: to:

- Eliminate superfluous relationships.
- Derive all parent-child relationships.
- Resolve multiple parentage.

The relationships represented in Figures 6.1 and 6.2 should be examined. The relationship between DEPARTMENT and EMPLOYEE is superfluous, since it can be derived from the relationship shown in Figure 6.2.

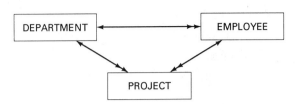

FIG. 6.1.   **Superfluous relationships.**

In deriving relationships, it is possible to derive a parent-child relationship from a given relationship. Let us examine the relationships represented in Figures 6.3 and 6.4.

We can derive a new relationship where either DEPARTMENT or EM-PLOYEE is the parent.

The significance of creating the parent-child relationship is illustrated as follows. Some information on the date that the employee joined the department, the results of performance reviews, promotions within the department, and job functions is stored. It can be seen that all of these stored attributes do not identify either the DEPARTMENT or EMPLOYEE entity, but identify the relationship between DEPARTMENT and EMPLOYEE. When this situation occurs, the key of the new entity is a combination of the keys of the two original entities.

The resolution of multiple parentage depends upon whether some parents are third normal form relations or a created relation. Very often, created entities are mainly needed for the physical implementation of the data model. When this is the case, and no data is lost by eliminating the created entity or by combining it with another entity, it is safe to opt for the elimination of the created entity and not the third normal form one.

The data model must be modified to conform to the constraints of the DBMS. For example, if the DBMS was Information Management System (IMS), the following constraints are present:

- There can be no more than 255 node types or segment types.
- There can be no more than 15 hierarchical levels.

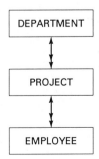

FIG. 6.2.   **Modifying relationships.**

FIG. 6.3.   The relationship between department and employee.

- A child segment type can have no more than two parents, a *physical parent* and a *logical parent.*
- A logical child cannot have a logical child.

On occasion, it may be desirous to add some relationships to the data model. The reason may be to add entities that provide better support for the data needs of the organization in the future. These should not be done in a way that would degrade the performance of the system.

6.3.2 Mapping to a Relational Data Model

As has been discussed before, the relational model consists of a number of relations or tables. In mapping the data model onto the constructs of the relational DBMS, a table for each entity in the model would be produced. The relationships between entities would show up as foreign keys in one of the related entities.

Mapping into a relational DBMS is a relatively easy process.

6.3.3 Mapping to a Network Data Model

In mapping a data model onto the constructs of the network DBMS, owner-member relationships within set types are derived. Some of the set types may be collapsed by combining entities or eliminating them after the normalization process.

The logical data base designers will have to pay more attention to performance considerations when mapping to a network data base than during similar phases of hierarchical or relational data base design.

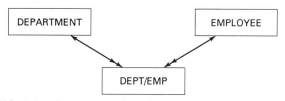

FIG. 6.4.   A representation of a parent-child relationship.

6.4 PHYSICAL DESIGN
OF DATA BASES

The physical model is a framework the data base to be stored on physical devices. The model must be constructed with every regard given to the performance of the resulting data base. An analysis of the physical model, average frequencies of occurrences of the groupings of the data elements, the expected space estimates, and time estimates for retrieving and maintaining the data must be done.

The data base designer may find it necessary to have multiple entry points into a data base, or to access a particular segment type with more than on key. To provide this type of access, it may be necessary to invert the segment on the keys, thereby posing some overhead on space and/or time. This is very often the price that must be paid to satisfy this particular business requirement.

The physical designer must have expertise in at least three areas:

- Knowledge of the DBMS functions.
- Understanding of the characteristics of direct access devices.
- Knowledge of the applications for which he intends to design storage formats.

The physical designer must know how the DBMS performs its specific functions. For example, in IBM's Information Management System (IMS) the designer must know the following:

1. That access to all segments, except when using secondary indexing, is through the root segment. Hence, remote segments should be confined to a few levels, and not spread out from left to right.
2. That retrieval from the data base is by segments. This means that a programmer may be presented with more data than is necessary. This often poses security problems for the installation. In this case, the trade-off is between too few and too many segments.
3. That frequently accessed segments should be kept at the top of the hierarchy, since all access is through the root of the hierarchy.
4. That one physical data base is based on one root segment. Hence, if one physical data base is expected to become too big, the designer should consider splitting it. However, the operational issues of backup and recovery must be taken int consideration for several physical data bases.
5. How to provide alternate paths to the data other than through the root segment. For example, it must be known that, with secondary indexing, IMS data base records can be accessed on data elements other than the primary key.

6.5 SELECTION OF
ACCESS METHODS

The way in which the data for subsequent retrieval is stored is often referred to as as the *file organization*. The way in which the data is retrieved is called the *access method*.

The types of access methods vary from manufacturer to manufacturer. The names also vary form DBMS to DBMS. The physical data base designer must be familiar with several access methods. However, because of the author's background in IMS, only those that are pertinent to IMS will be discussed.

IMS allows the designer to define nine different types of data bases. These are as follows:

Data Base Type	Group	Access Method
HSAM	Sequential	Hierarchical Sequential
SHSAM	Sequential	Simple Hierarchical Sequential
HISAM	Sequential	Hierarchical Indexed Sequential
SHISAM	Sequential	Simple Hierarchical Indexed Sequential
HDAM	Direct	Hierarchical Direct
HIDAM	Direct	Hierarchical Indexed Direct
MSDB	Direct	Main Storage
DEDB	Direct	Data Entry

6.5.1 Hierarchical Sequential Data Bases

HSAM data bases use the sequential method of storing data. All data base records and all segments within each data base record are physically adjacent in storage.

HSAM data sets are loaded with root segments in ascending key sequence, and dependent segments in hierarchic sequence. A key field does not have to be defined in root segments. However, segments must be presented to the load program in the order in which they are to be loaded. HSAM data sets use a fixed-length, unblocked record format (RECFM = F), which means that the logical record length is the same as the physical block size

HSAM data bases can only be updated by rewriting them. They are appropriate primarily for low-use files. For example, audit trails, statistical reports, or files containing historical or archival data.

Segments in an HSAM data base are loaded in the order in which they are presented to the load program. All segments within a data base record should be presented in hierarchic sequence. In the data set, a data base record is stored in one or more consecutive blocks. If there is not enough space left in the block to store the next segment, the remaining space is filled with zeros and the next segment is stored in the next consecutive block.

Figure 6.5 illustrates the HSAM data base records sequence.

Figure 6.6 illustrates how the HSAM data base records would be stored.

6.5.2 Hierarchical Indexed Sequential Data Bases

In an HISAM data base, as with HSAM data bases, segments in each data base record are related through physical adjacency in storage. Unlike HSAM, however,

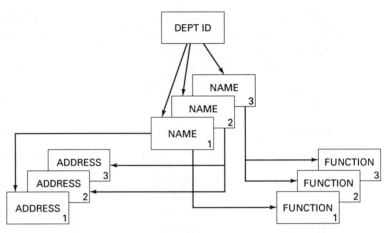

FIG. 6.5.   Representation of the HSAM data base in hierarchic sequence.

a unique sequence field in each root segment must be defined. These sequence fields are then used to construct an index to root segments in the data base.

HISAM is typically used for data bases that require direct access to data base records and sequential processing of segments in a data base record. It's a good candidate for data bases with the following characteristics:

- Most data base records are about the same size
- The data base does not consist of relatively few root segments and a large number of dependent segments
- Applications don't require a heavy volume of root segments inserted after the data base is initially loaded
- Deletion of data base records is minimal

HISAM data base records are stored in two data sets. The first, called the *primary data set,* contains an index and all segments in a data base record that can fit into one logical record. The index provides direct access to the root segment. The second data set, called the *overflow data set,* contains all segments in the data base record that cannot fit in the primary data set.

Figure 6.7 illustrates the HISAM data base records sequence.

Figure 6.8 illustrates how HISAM data base records are stored.

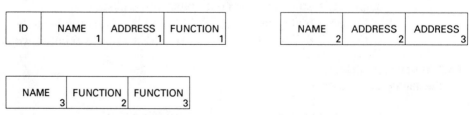

FIG. 6.6.   The storage of HSAM records.

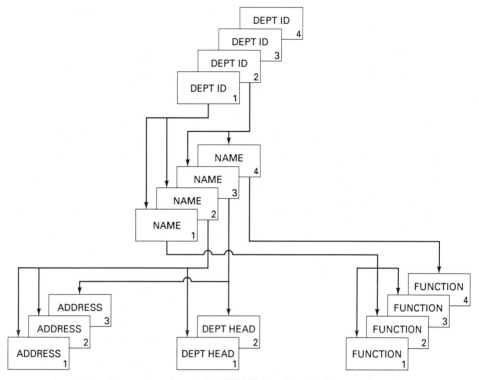

FIG. 6.7.   Representation of the HISAM data base in hierarchic sequence.

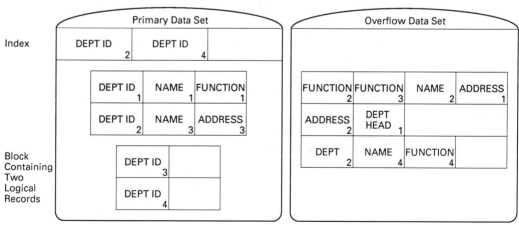

FIG. 6.8.   The storage of HISAM records.

There are several things that should be known about the storage of HISAM data base records:

- The logical record length of both the primary and overflow data set are defined by the user.
- The size of the control interval or block are defined by the user.
- Each data base record starts at the beginning of a logical record in the primary data set.
- Segments in a data base record cannot be split and stored across two logical records.

6.5.3 Hierarchical Direct (HD) Data Bases

Hierarchical direct data bases differ from sequentially organized data bases in two important ways. First, they use a direct method of storing data; that is, the hierarchic sequence of segments in the data base is maintained by having segments point to one another. Except for a few special cases, each segment has one or more direct-address pointers in its prefix. When direct-address pointers are used, data base records and segments can be stored anywhere in the data base. Their position, once stored, is fixed. Instead, pointers are updated to reflect processing changes.

HD data bases also differ from sequentially organized ones in that space in HD data bases can be reused. If part or all of a data base record is deleted, the deleted space can be reused when new data base records or segments are inserted.

HDAM data bases are used when direct access to data base records is needed. A randomizing module provides fast access to the root segment.

HIDAM data bases are used when both random and sequential access to data base records and random access to paths or segments in a data base record is needed. Access to root segments is not as fast as with HDAM, because the HIDAM index data base has to be searched for a root segment's address. However, because the index keeps the address of root segments stored in key sequence, data base records can be processed sequentially.

The next few diagrams illustrate how hierarchical direct data bases are stored and processed.

In hierarchic pointers (Fig. 6.9), each pointer points from one segment to the next in either forward or forward and backward hierarchic sequence.

In physical-child first pointers (Fig. 6.10), each pointer points from a parent to the first child or dependent segment. It should be noticed that no pointers exist to connect occurrences of the same segment type under a parent.

In physical-twin forward pointers (Fig. 6.11), each segment occurrence of a given segment type under the same parent points forward to the next segment occurrence.

HDAM data bases consist of two parts: a root addressable area and an overflow

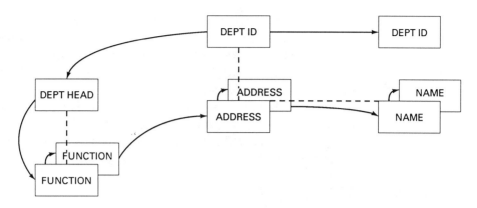

FIG. 6.9.   Hierarchic forward pointers.

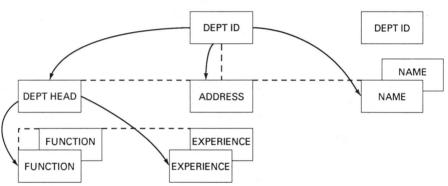

FIG. 6.10.   Physical child first pointers.

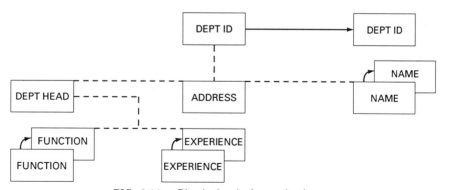

FIG. 6.11.   Physical twin forward pointers.

area. The root addressable area contains root segments and is the primary storage area for dependent segments in a data base record. The overflow area is for the storage of dependent segments that don't fit into the root addressable area.

Root segments in HDAM data bases must have a key field, although the key field doesn't have to be unique.

An HIDAM data base is actually composed of two data bases. One is for storage of the data base records, the other for the HIDAM index.

Root segments in HIDAM data bases must have a unique key field. This is because an index entry exists for each root segment, based on the root's key.

6.6 SUMMARY

This chapter dealt with the logical and physical design aspects of data base development. In the logical design phase, it was discovered that the primary output was a data model, with the constructs of the relevant DBMS superimposed. In the physical design phase, it was indicated that the important steps were calculating space and time estimates, selecting access methods, and learning the mechanics of the data base.

The chapter discussed, in some detail, the access methods of IMS, a hierarchical DBMS.

Finally, the chapter served as a forerunner to Chapter 7, where the planning and control of the data base will be discussed.

PART 2

MANAGEMENT OF THE DATA BASE ENVIRONMENT

7

Management, Planning, and Control of the Data Base

7.1 INTRODUCTION

In an earlier chapter, the premise was established that data is a resource, in much the same manner as employees, products, natural resources, finances, and other material products or resources.

In the same chapter, Information Resource Management (IRM) was defined as a discipline that deals with planning for, allocating, maintaining and conserving, prudently exploiting, effectively employing, and integrating the data resource.

This chapter deals with three aspects of IRM. It deals with the effective management of the data resource. It emphasizes the fact that, in order to effectively manage data, it is necessary to obtain as much information about the data resource as is possible. It deals with planning for the data resource. In planning for this resource, the strategic, tactical, and operational aspects of IRM planning are emphasized. In the area of the control of the data resource, IRM deals with establishing lines of authority and responsibility for the data. It emphasizes the importance of having common procedures for collecting, updating, and maintaining the data. Finally, it establishes that, in order to control the data resource, the organization must evaluate, mediate between, and reconcile the conflicting needs and perogatives of its functional departments.

7.2 MANAGEMENT OF THE DATA RESOURCE

In order to manage data effectively as a resource, it is necessary to obtain as much information about the data resource as possible. There must be stringent procedures for collecting, maintaining, and using the resource. The next several sections of this chapter will discuss various tools that can be used in the effective management of the data resource.

7.2.1 The Data Dictionary

The data dictionary may be defined as an organized reference to the data content of an organization's programs, systems, databases, collections of all files, or manual records.

 The data dictionary may be maintained manually or by a computer. Sometimes, the term 'data dictionary' may refer to a software product that is utilized to maintain a dictionary data base. The data dictionary will contain names, descriptions, and definitions of the organization's data resource.

7.2.2 The Data Dictionary as a Management Tool

The data dictionary is perhaps the most important tool that information resource managers have at their disposal. The data dictionary allows management to document and support application development and to assist in designing and controlling the data base environment. It allows managers to set standards and to monitor adherence to those standards.

 In the data base environment, the data dictionary can be used to document the single-user view of the organization's data, or several integrated views. It can document the related data models of those views, the logical data bases that result from those views, and the physical representation of those logical models.

 The organization can store complete representations of its data architecture in the data dictionary. This data architecture can be used to indicate how adequately the data resource supports the business functions of the organization, and also show what data the company will need to support its long-range plans for expansion.

 The dictionary allows information managers to respond quickly to upper-level management's needs for data in a decision-support environment. It supports the organization's need for consistant data definitions and usage.

 The data dictionary can be used to indicate management's desire to control access to the organization's data resource. Managers can now state who can access the data, and the level of access assigned to the individual. They can use the data dictionary, in connection with the operating system, to deny access to unauthorized individuals.

 The data dictionary can provide managers and other users with concise definitions of entities and data items that are important to the organization. It can indicate where data is used, what area uses it, how it is used, and other dependencies on that data.

Management can indicate, via the dictionary, who is responsible for changing the characteristics of the data resource and the procedures for effecting the change. On the other hand, managers can use the dictionary to control changes to the data resource and can readily assess the effect on systems, programs, and user operations when such changes are made.

7.2.3 The Data Base as a Management Tool

Today's highly competitive business climate, characterized by more educated consumers and shorter product cycles, forces companies to be information-driven. Corporate decision makers derive information by analyzing raw data, gathered internally or externally, in a particular business context. Therefore, to be successful, a company must ensure that this raw data is capture and readily available for analysis in various forms. If such data is not easily accessible, various levels of support must be built before meaningful information can be obtained.

Various methods have evolved over the past two decades for facilitating data resource management. When first introduced, Data Base Management Systems (DBMS) were thought to offer a panacea to the growing lack of control over company data resources.

The data base can be defined as a collection of interrelated data items processable by one or more applications systems. The data base permits common data to be integrated and shared between corporate functional units, and provides for flexibility of data organization. It facilitates the addition of data to an existing data base, without the modification of existing application programs. This data independence is achieved by removing the direct association between the applications program and the physical storage of data.

The advantages of the data base are:

- Consistency, through use of the same data by all corporate parts.
- Applications program independence from data sequence and structure.
- Reduction and control of redundant data.
- Reduction in applications development costs, storage costs, and processing costs.

Data base technology has permitted information resource managers to organize data around subjects that interest the company. It has allowed for data sharing among divergent parts of the organization. It has introduced new methods of managing data; and new and sophisticated logical and physical design methodologies. By having a central pool of data, the organization can now secure the resource more effeciently and in more cost-effective ways. Access to the data can be more readily controlled, while making it available to a wider audience of diverse users.

The technology has allowed management, through Decision Support Systems (DSS), to more readily adjust to the changing environment of their respective businesses, and to reduce the impact of these changes on the organization's economy.

7.2.4 Managing the Corporate Data Base

Effective management of the corporate data base requires that the following activities be addressed consistently and logically:

- Planning—The corporate data base must be planned according to the specific needs of the company.
- Organization—A data-driven company requires new organizational entities.
- Acquisition—Once the corporate data base has been planned, the needed data must be acquired.
- Maintenance and control—The data in the corporate data base must be securely, accurately, and completely maintained. In addition, proper control must be exercised over access to the data base. Data ownership, use, and custodianship issues must also be addressed.
- Usage—The corporate data base must be available to all authorized users in the company.

Planning. Planning entails the preparation of all corporate data models. This is best achieved through interviews with the department heads of each functional area in the company. These managers should be asked to determine what data influences their functional areas and what information is required to successfully operate and manage their departments. After all of the interviews are completed, the collection of data items must be analyzed and distilled into a model that can be understood, presented, and accepted by corporate management. This analysis should include a determination of the source of the data, as well as its characteristics and interrelationships with other data items. This corporate data model must then be compared with currently held and maintained data. The differences between what is currently available and what is ultimately required determines what data must be collected.

Organization. There are two distinct aspects of organizing the corporate data base. The first is the business aspect; identifying which data is relevant to the company, its source and method of capture, and the interrelationships among the data items. The second is the technical aspect: storing data on computer-readable media in a form readily accessible by the corporate decision makers. The business tasks of organizing the corporate data base required both the creation of the relatively new position of Chief Information Officer (CIO), and the more traditional data administration function.

The CIO is the executive in charge of the information systems department, and is responsible for formulating an information strategy that includes all systems development, computer operations, and communications planning and operation.

The data administration function links computer systems and the business functions that they are designed to serve. The group responsible for data administration builds and maintains the corporate data model. A properly constructed data model places the system to be developed into a proper business perspective. This model is instrumental in the preparation of the information systems department's strategic plan.

Acquisition. In a data-driven organization, information strategy is derived from the corporate data model. Systems planned for development should provide either information or a level of service that was previously unavailable. In a typical systems development project, a major part of the effort is spent in acquiring and storing the data that is used to produce the required information.

Although data analysis and design is defined as a separate activity in the definition of data resource management, application programs to collect and validate data items, and add them to the appropriate data base, must still be written. The interactions among systems development, data administration, and data base administration must be in place to ensure that the corporate database effectively acquires data.

Maintenance and control. Maintenance tasks include making changes to the corporate data model, reflecting these changes in the data dictionary, and properly communicating the changes to all of the users who must know the model's current status. Given the degree of data independence that can be achieved in today's DBMS's, changes to the data base should not necessitate changes to application programs. However, the addition of new data items, and changes or deletions to existing data items, must be controlled as vigorously as changes to applications systems. That is, the change control principles applied to applications programs must be applied to changes in data definitions used by these programs.

Data security issues are critical in data-driven organizations. the data is used and relied on by all corporate users, including high-level decision makers. Procedures must be established that define which individuals, and what level of access, should be granted. Unauthorized access must be detected and reported. The cause of the infraction also must be determined, and action taken to prevent its recurrence.

The distinction must be made between data owners—those with update authority—and data users—those with read-only access or limited update authority.

The computer operations group is the custodian of all data. This group must ensure that proper monitoring is performed and that backup and recovery procedures are in place and functioning. The data administrator should also have sufficient authority to arbitrate any ownership disputes between rival users.

Maintenance and control activities should also monitor systems performance and the time required to access needed data items. The data base administration group should monitor system performance and take whatever corrective action is needed to provide an adequate level of response to users or systems requiring access to particular data items.

Usage. Procedures that clearly define how to use the data base must be established. First, potential users must know what data exists. Then, tools must be provided to enable users to easily access selected data items. For example, query languages that provide flexible data base access, and allow what-if questions to be presented and answered, are implemented in many companies. Another area of great potential is the ability to interface selected data items with business software tools. These interfaces provide users with more meaningful presentations of the extracted information.

The delivery vehicle used to bring the data to the users must also be considered. Many companies have established information centers to provide a user-friendly environment for data access. This access may be provided through interactive query languages that enable users to view results either on-line, or through batch report generators that enable users to obtain preformatted printed reports.

Downloading segments of the data base to a microcomputer is another method of information delivery that is becoming more common. The microcomputer environment typically provides the user with interactive access to the data, as well as easy-to-use and powerful software. With the continuing emergence of local area networks (LANS), more and more data will be downloaded to microcomputers for use by the end-user community.

7.2.5 The Data Model as a Management Tool

A data model is defined as a logical representation of a collection of data elements and the associations among those data elements. A data model can be used to represent data usage throughout an organization, or can represent a single data base structure. A data model is to data what a logical data flow diagram is to a process.

The data model can be used by management to:

- develop new systems
- maintain existing systems
- develop data structures for the entire organization
- prioritize the data needs of the organization
- assist in planning for expansion into new markets or business areas
- delegate authority for data usage
- classify data by data areas or business functions
- determine the security needs of the data and implement protection mechanisms

The development of new systems. Data models are fast becoming a very important tool in the development of new systems in an organization. The advent of new structured design methodologies, especially data-driven methodologies, saw the birth of data models as tools for systems development. The traditional approach to developing computer systems focuses on the processes to be performed, particularly with operational-type systems. However, process-oriented system designs generally do not fulfill subsequent tactical or strategic information needs. In many cases, information requests go unanswered, either because the source data does not exist, or because custom building software that supports ad hoc inquiries is too costly and time-consuming. This lack of accurate information is a major disadvantage of many conventional systems.

The data resource management approach overcomes this limitation by focusing on data and information requirements during systems planning and building. The data model now becomes the vehicle by which applications systems are built, while addressing these limitations.

The maintanence of existing systems. It has now been determined that 80 percent of an organization's programming resources is expended for maintenance of existing systems. This expenditure is consumed by programmers trying to determine where changes should be made to existing systems and what data is best suited to test the modified programs. The expenditure may even occur before the changes are made. Programmers may spend, depending upon their experience, a considerable amount of time determining how the application meets the requirements of the business function. This expenditure in time and financial resources can be minimized if there are data models of all existing systems in place.

The programmers can determine, from the data models, the section or user view that must be modified. Then, with the data model section or user view as a guide, the parts of the applications programs that must be changed can be more easily identified, and programming maintenance expenditure would be less costly.

The development of data structures for the organization. The organization, by undertaking a Business Systems Plan (BSP), can identify the business processes and data classes required for the design of data bases for its informational needs. Various charts showing the relationship between business processes and classes of data can be prepared. This relationship is the backbone of the data architecture for the organization. The data architecture, in turn, is obtained through a single data model or set of data models.

The prioritization of the data needs of the organization. It is impossible, in most organizations, to implement systems that will satisfy all of their data needs all at once. Priorities must be set, and phased implementation of these systems undertaken. The data model can show what data is available, where it is available, and where is it needed. Data managers can use this information to determine the cost and complexity of the implementation of systems, and hence prioritize the implementation of these systems.

Assistance in planning for the expansion of business. Whenever an organization expands its business into new markets or business areas, data is needed to aid or even implement the expansion. Data models are very useful tools that management can use to determine what data is needed and where it can be obtained for the expansion program.

The delegation of authority for data usage. Data models can indicate to an organization which business function uses what data. They can also be used to indicate the common uses and functions of corporate data. Corporate management can use this information to delegate authority for data usage throughout the organization. Managers can also use this information to control access, on a need-to-know basis, to the corporate data.

The classification of data by data areas. Data is very often classified by the business function it serves. For example, data that serves an accounting function is very often classified as accounting data. Data models, by showing the relationship between business functions and business entities (data), can assist in the proper classification of corporate data.

Determining the security needs of data. Data models allow an organization to determine what data is available, who uses it, and where it is being used. They allow the organization to determine the common usage of data and the parameters that are needed to allow data usage across organizational boundaries. Armed with this knowledge, an organization can now plan for its data security needs. It can determine what protection mechanisms are needed to control access to the data, and the level of authorization to be given to users of corporate data.

7.2.6 Data Flow Diagrams as Management Tools

Data flow diagrams can assist systems analysts in determining where data is being held from one transaction to the next, or stored permanently, because it describes some aspect of the world outside of the system. They indicate how the data flows from process to process. They assist analysts in determining what immediate accesses to each data store will be needed by the user.

Data flow diagrams are powerful tools that can be used by organizations to develop process-flow archtectures for their environment. Management can use this tool to determine where data is created, where it is being used, and who uses the informational contents.

Management can use data flow diagrams to build complete data bases to store the required data for users' needs. They can use the processes to transform flows of data. The processes can be decomposed into functions and activities from which programs can be coded to manipulate the data stores.

Data flow diagrams are currently being used on a world-wide basis as the major output from process-driven structured systems analysis and development. Several organizations are using data flow diagrams as a output of a basic Business Systems Plan (BSP). Data flow diagrams are also being used by several organizations to demonstrate and illustrate their corporate data needs.

Management can use the ability to break down processes into several levels to determine the operational processing requirements of each data store in the process architecture. For example, one organization is currently using data flow diagrams to determine whether operational processing, such as sorting, dumping to other storage media, deleting of files, and the creation of back-up files, is consuming too much of the corporation's operational budgets and time. This same organization is using data flow diagrams to illustrate where various reports are distributed to other users, whether current users should have access to the reports, and where reports are produced but never distributed.

Management can use existing data flow diagrams to audit the corporate data dictionary for completeness and currency. For example, a complete data dictionary should have data regarding all of the processes and data stores that exist in the organization. By checking the data dictionary content against existing data flow diagrams, the completeness of the data dictionary can be determined. The assumption here is that the data flow diagrams are in themselves complete, and represent the entire information and process architecture of the corporation.

Data flow diagrams can be used to create functional specifications for systems development. The data flow diagram shows the sources and distinctions of data, and hence indicate the boundaries of the system. It identifies and names the logical functions, the names of the data elements that connect one function to another, and the data stores that each function accesses. Each data flow is analyzed, and the structures and the definitions of its component data elements are stored in the data dictionary. Each logical function may be broken down into a more detailed data flow diagram. The contents of each data store is analyzed and stored in the data dictionary.

These documents make up a comprehensive account of a system, which can be used by management to build systems or prioritize the building of systems. The documents and the data flow diagrams may also prove very useful in the maintenance of existing systems.

Finally, data flow diagrams can be used by systems designers to prepare functional specifications that are:

- Well-understood and fully agreed to by users
- Used to set out the logical requirements of the system without dictating a physical implementation
- Useful in expressing preferences and trade-offs

Several organizations have attested to the fact that data flow diagrams can prevent very costly errors in systems development. Figure 7.1 is an example of a data flow diagram.

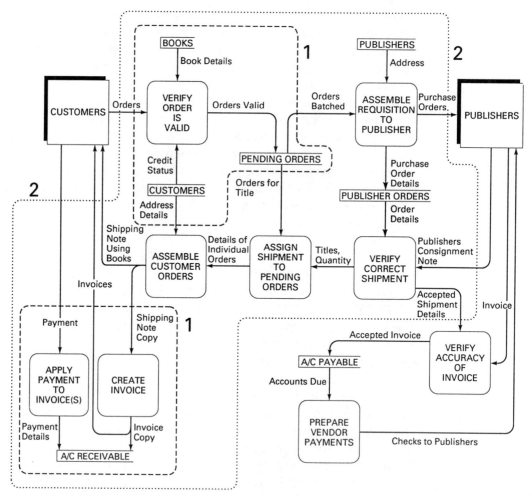

FIG. 7.1.   Illustration of a data flow diagram.

7.2.7 Managing Information through the Utilization of CASE Tools

More and more organizations are looking to Computer-Aided Software Engineering (CASE) tools to improve the effectiveness of analysts and designers, increase the role of end-users in systems design, reduce programming and maintenance time, and manage data more effectively.

CASE is the automation of software development. It is a combination of software tools and systems development methodologies. CASE is different from earlier software technologies in that it focuses on the entire software productivity problem, not just on implementation solutions. It attacks software productivity problems at both ends of the life cycle, by automating many analysis and design tasks, as well as with program implementation and maintenance tasks.

CASE offers full support for the systems development life cycle. In the analysis phase, it allows the designer to collect user requirements either through conventional interview methods or by the use of Structured English. The collected user requirements are entered into a CASE repository or data dictionary and become the input to the design phase. The output from the design phase can be data models, such as entity-relationship diagrams, or data flow diagrams. The CASE tools have the ability to decompose the data flow diagrams down to several levels, and to balance the data stores at each level. The outputs are checked against the data dictionary entries for accuracy, consistency, and completeness.

Most of the tools have a prototyping capability and can create screens of the user requirements and models of the systems, so that users can review the design at a very early stage of systems development. During prototyping, simulated reports can be produced that reflect the actual reports required by the users.

CASE tools use the entries in the data dictionary and the processes from the design phase not only to develop programming specifications for application programmers, but some tools can even generate the actual program code compatible with standards for several programming languages.

At the moment, the major weakness of the tools is in their inability to maintain program code and changes to existing systems over the life of the system. Several manufacturers of CASE tools are now developing solutions to this problem, and the answers may not be long in coming.

These have become very important tools for managers to use in their efforts to manage data more effectively, and to prudently exploit the data resource. They now represent the most rapidly growing sector of the software industry. CASE tools—what they are and how they should be selected, is the topic of Chapter 10.

7.2.8 Managing Information through Reverse Engineering

Reverse engineering, in the present area of discussion, is defined as the act of taking unstructured programs or systems not designed with one of the current structured design methodologies, and either structuring the programs or producing output more appropriate to the structured Systems Development Life Cycle (SDLC).

Reverse engineering accomplishes the following:

- It produces programs that are structured, and thereby less costly, both in time and money, to maintain.
- It enhances the quality of programs, program documentation, and informational content.
- It increases the useful life of program code and identifies sections of programs that can be reused as subroutines.
- It removes or identifies unreachable or unexecutable codes in programs.
- It indicates problem areas in unstructured programs that could be responsible for seemingly inexplicable processing behavior.

Although most of the effort of reverse engineering now centers on producing structured program code from unstructured code, a considerable amount of effort is being expended in producing output more appropriate to a structured SDLC. For example, there are efforts being undertaken to produce entity-relationship (E-R) diagrams from the data division of COBOL programs. These E-R diagrams are then used, along with the major processes defined by the COBOL programs, to populate data dictionaries, produce logical and physical design schemas, provide better documentation for programming specifications and maintenance, and build relevant data bases. Managers can now use the data dictionary content, the documentation, and the data bases to more effectively manage the data resource.

7.2.9 Project Management Tools and the Management of Data

There are now several automated project management tools on the market, which seek to aid in the development of systems and, indirectly, in the management of data.

Project management tools are used in the following areas:

- Project planning
- Project duration
- Costing
- Manpower scheduling
- Manpower allocation
- Project reporting

7.3 PLANNING FOR THE DATA RESOURCE

Planning for the data resource is done at three levels: the strategic, tactical, and operational.

7.3.1 Strategic Planning

This planning area defines the data environment's mission and objective in achieving the goals of the organization. The strategic plan is driven by the current and future information needs of the business. Strategic planning helps businesses share the data resource.

The strategic data plan defines the organization's data requirements, and states the benefits of data resource management and the ways in which it differs from data base technology management. The strategic plan serves as a baseline for data resource management and directs all subsequent data-related activities.

The strategic plan defines the target toward which all subsequent data-related activity is directed.

Contents of the strategic plan. The strategic plan should address the broadest context under which data sharing will exist, and should contain the following sections:

- The purpose of the data resource.
- Goals for supporting the information strategies of the organization.
- Strategies that pursue the goals.
- Factors critical to successfully achieving the goals.
- Constraints imposed on the data environment.
- The concepts of data resource management.
- The resources needed to manage data.

7.3.2 Tactical Planning

Tactical planning identifies a resource and directs the way in which it will be managed to achieve the goals set forth in the strategic plan. Because each resource is to be managed in its own life cycle, each should ideally be governed by its own plan. The tactical planning window is 12 to 18 months, with a review cycle of 9 to 12 months.

7.3.3 Operational Planning

This planning area describes the details of the tactical plan and identifies the tasks to be carried out in a scheduled time frame, the expected output, and the assigned responsibilities. The operational planning window is 3 to 9 months, depending on the size of the project.

Mission statement. This reflects an overall direction for data resource management from a single, high-level perspective. It defines the scope of the data environment. For example, a mission statement may read as follows: To provide data about shared corporate entities to all regional offices in a timely and controlled manner.

Goals. This identifies expected results to be gained in that domain. For example, a goal of data resource management may be to build a strategic data architecture that will ensure the integrity of data as it is integrated across application systems.

Strategies. These are general statements of direction for achieving data resource management goals. Strategies are generally applied across goals to identify how the goals will be achieved. For example, a strategy for data resource management may be to train systems staff and end-users in data-oriented systems design and data base development, or to provide effective data security with minimal interruption to end-user service.

Critical success factors. These are broad statements of achievements in data resource management. For example, a critical success factor may be the management of data through a data dictionary. Success is achieved with the implementation and effective use of the data dictionary.

Constraints. Data resource management may be constrained by the evolution of
the business, the state of the technology in the environment, and the availability of
staff. Current business operations and the role of information in the organization's
planning may force constraints on the scope of data resource management.

Planning for the data resource must include: acquisition of data through application systems, employment and exploitation of data through end-user reports,
maintenance of data through the technology tools, and disposition of the data depending on the life cycle of the business subject matter. The deletion of the data
element is determined by its relationship to other elements.

Planning for the data resource must identify the tools used to manage the data
resource, including: Data Base Management Systems; data dictionaries; data
modelling tools; CASE tools; and data base auditing, journalling, and recovery
tools.

7.4 CONTROLLING
THE DATA RESOURCE

The third component of information resource management is the control of the
data resource. Although the other two components, management and planning,
were discussed first, this is no indication of their relative importance in the trium-
verate.

Management control of the data resource includes the following:

- Common procedures for access control to the data.
- Establishing lines of authority and responsibility for the data.
- Common procedures for collecting, updating, and maintaining the data.
- Common formats and procedures for data definition.
- Identifying entities that are important to the enterprise.
- Evaluating, mediating, and reconciling the conflicting needs and prerogatives
  of functional departments.
- Ensuring the auditability of the data and all transactions against the data.
- Control of the data in order to measure and evaluate the corporation and
  predict its reaction to change in its environment and in its own internal
  organization.

The above list, although quite extensive, is by no means all-inclusive. It will be
left to the readers to expand on this list, and also to research the various activities
that must be performed to materialize each item in the list.

8

Concepts of Data Dictionaries

8.1 INTRODUCTION

Over the past several years, the data dictionary has been used as a tool by data administrators to document and maintain the names and definitions of the data items in the data base. However, with the increasing recognition of data as a corporate resource and the need to manage these resources more efficiently, data administrators are putting the data dictionary to several different uses.

8.2 DATA DICTIONARY AS A GLOSSARY OF DEFINITIONS

One use of the data dictionary is as a glossary of terms, whether about the entire organization, or for entire systems. The glossary allows users to communicate with one another using common terms and definitions.

The data dictionary can also be used as a glossary of data items. In this case, a few lines or few paragraphs are dedicated to defining the data items used in the data base environment.

8.3 DATA DICTIONARY AS A SYSTEM DEVELOPMENT AND MAINTENANCE TOOL

The data dictionary can be very effective when used as a tool to support structured analysis and design. It can be used to document data items, data flow, and process definitions. As such, it is an efficient way of portraying system design details to the user.

The data dictionary can also be used to generate file, segment, and record definitions for a variety of programming languages. By doing so, control of program data definitions can be centralized. This will ensure consistency of data use, and inhibit data redundancy.

Because the control of data use can be centralized, the data dictionary can be a very effective tool in change-control management. The data dictionary is the origin of all data definitions, and so any new data requirements must have the knowledge and approval of the data administration (Durell, 1983).

Because the dictionary enforces consistency of data naming and format variation, it significantly reduces the cost of program maintenance.

8.4 DATA DICTIONARY AS A SUPERIOR DOCUMENTATION MEDIUM

Documentation stored in a data dictionary is available to anyone who has access to a computer terminal (and is properly authorized for access). The automated search and cross-referencing tools of a data dictionary can span multiple programs, systems, data bases, report definitions, form definitions, or any other entity type.

The data dictionary can be used to generate the source program data definitions; the data portion of the program is actually derived from the documentation.

8.5 CASE HISTORIES OF DATA DICTIONARY USE

Company A is a leading energy company in New York City. This company's data base administration department has been evolving since 1976. The stated objectives of the DBA are:

- Data is an important shared resource that should be managed and controlled, just like other major corporate resources.
- Knowledge as to how data and information are generated and used should become widely disseminated.
- Control should be exercised over the quality of the data resource, to increase its effective utilization.

The DBA function exerts control over the data resources through management control of applications development, test, and production environments. The company's DBA function sees its proper role as a full-time participant in the planning, design, and operation of data base systems, with a view to ensuring that adequate features and appropriate data safeguards are provided.

In all of these efforts, the manager of data base administration sees the data dictionary as the primary tool for this function. The data dictionary is being used to organize the collection, storage, and retrieval of information about data.

8.5.1 Data Dictionary Use at Company A

The facilities of company A's data dictionary are useful to all system development projects, non-data base as well as data base. The main thrust is to capture information describing data items and their attributes, highlighting their interrelationships. Functional analysis is also supported by the dictionary, based on its ability to define business activities in a machine-readable form.

The data dictionary is a tool that enables the DBA function to:

- clarify and design data structures.
- avoid unwanted data redundancies.
- generate accurate and dependable data definitions.
- assess the impact of proposed computer system changes.
- enforce standards related to data.

Because of the interest in management uses of data, the DBA function looks to see what management-type data can be provided by each new application system. The DBA introduces appropriate integrated data base designs, which minimize the need for special processing to make that data suitable for current and future management uses.

8.5.2 Example of Management Uses of the Data Dictionary

An example of management use of the data dictionary is the Human Resources Information System (HURIS). Now under development, this system will establish a single source of people data within the company, servicing such applications functions as payroll, employee relations, benefit plans, and so on. In addition to their on-going review function and assistance in data base design and installation, the DBA function developed a control monitor that supports an unusually flexible security apparatus, as well an an on-line report request and distribution system for end users.

8.5.3 Company A's Approach to Using the Data Dictionary

The first step in company A's approach to using the data dictionary was to acquire the basic dictionary capabilities and train the DBA staff members in their use.

Then, corporate policies were established that required dictionary use for all data base projects. The DBA is now in the process of developing additional tools, procedures, and educational materials to enhance the usefulness of the data dictionary.

Ultimately, the DBA function must impose a discipline on data content and not just its form. The staff must coordinate the definition of all data that crosses departmental boundaries; for data that is used only by one department, there is less need to impose standards. The DBA function acts to clean up the existing data definitions and then monitor all additions, deletions, and changes to these definitions.

In the long run, the monitoring and editing of data definitions are essential if data resources are to become truly sharable. The editing of key data definitions found in all application systems is very large undertaking, so this step should be approached somewhat cautiously.

8.5.4 Company A's Use of the Data Dictionary for Business Planning

An area of current interest is the mechanism by which the DBA function can support business planning. Beginning with the business objectives, the business processes needed to support these objectives are identified and recorded in the dictionary. Next, the information needs of those business processes are identified and recorded in the dictionary, and support the locating of data-sharing opportunities. All of this data—data about business opportunities, processes, information, and sharing potential—can be made more manageable in the context of a data dictionary.

These planning processes are not yet fully realized at company A. They depend on developing the DBA's own understanding of these methods and educating the corporate community in the advantages of the formal definitions of information entities.

Company A has thus embarked on a broad program for the management and control of its data resources (Canning, 1981).

8.5.5 Data Dictionary Use at Company B

Company B is a large telephone company in a large Canadian city. This company's data administration department has been evolving since 1977.

Company B has had the on-line IBM Data Dictionary for several years, but is not making extensive use of its capabilities. The data administration area uses the dictionary as a passive tool to maintain details of the data base control blocks, data base definitions, and the program specification blocks. The dictionary facilitates the management of several test and production versions of data base definitions. The company has captured some descriptions of major databases and files and their fields, but has not progressed to the point of describing in detail all major data bases and files.

The company reported that the IBM dictionary was not particularly user-friendly and has been relegated, almost solely, to use by the technical database support personnel. The company's information center personnel did not find the dictionary easy to use, and found that the standard reports produced were somewhat lacking in user appeal. They found the screens used for input/query were not, however, easily changed and were definitely geared to more technical users than those which the information center supports.

8.5.6 Company B's Use of the Extensibility Feature of the Data Dictionary

The extensibility features of the IBM data dictionary allow the user to code, debug, and document development systems and their programs. Entire batch or on-line transaction-driven systems can be developed using the extensibility features. However, company B is not currently using these features.

The company is currently involved in the production of a corporate data model. Data administration is now considering placing the results of the data model into the extensibility categories in the dictionary, as the data model results are of prime importance to the management of data within the corporation.

Company B feels that no one dictionary on the market handles the areas of production control block and data definition program code, data analysis by-products, and data base design assistance requirements well enough to be the sole tool used in those areas. It is for these reasons that the data dictionary at company B is not used extensively.

8.6 THE CONCEPT OF METADATA

In order to manage data as a resource that is shared by users at various levels in an organization, it is essential that information about data (metadata) be clearly specified, easily accessible, and well-controlled. The first step in this process is to identify and describe those data objects that are of interest to the organization and about which the organization wishes to store information (Leong-Hong and Plagman, 1982). The data used to identify and describe the objects is entered into the data dictionary system as metadata.

Metadata should not be confused with the user data or actual data that is stored in the dictionary. For example, the metadata for an attribute CUSTOMER NAME will describe the entry for that attribute as "the name of a person who conducts business with the organization," whereas the user data will give the name of the customer (e.g., "TOM CLARK").

An example of the metadata for an attribute in the data dictionary follows (Brathwaite, 1983):

- ATTRIBUTE NAME—a symbolic or descriptive name conventionally used to identify the ATTRIBUTE and its representations. Attribute names are used as the preferred method of referencing attributes.
- ALIASES—a list of names used as alternate identifiers for the attribute and its representations.
- ATTRIBUTE DESCRIPTION—a free-form narrative containing a description of the attribute and its various representations. The description contains a concise definition of the attribute in a form suitable for use in a glossary.
- ATTRIBUTE FUNCTION—a free-form narrative describing the corporate interest in the attribute and its physical representations. The narrative describes the purpose and use of the attribute as it relates to corporate objectives and the business functions used to achieve them.
- DEFINITION UPDATE SOURCE—a composite structure identifying the individuals or groups who updated a dictionary entry and the dates on which those updates were made. A single occurrence of the structure is recorded for each update. It takes the form:

SOURCE (DATE)

where SOURCE is a three-character field identifying the person or group who submitted the definition modification.
- DEFINITION ACCEPTANCE STATUS—a composite structure identifying the project teams or organizational groups who created the definition or who must be informed of its subsequent updates. The structure is used as the basis for propagating definition changes to support groups who may be affected by the proposed modifications.
- DEFINITION RESPONSIBILITY—a set of references to the organizational groups charged with the responsibility for the accuracy and ongoing integrity of a definition. The references are used to establish a relationship between the dictionary entry and the organizational groups identified as the definitive source of information about the attribute's meaning and use.
- STANDARD REPRESENTATION ENTRIES—a composite structure listing and the physical characteristics of the representation defined to be the standard representation of attribute values.

Standard representation attributes are documented in the following form:

Standard Representation Attributes

JUSTIFICATION	—LEFT
CODING STRUCTURE	—ALPHABETIC
DATA LENGTH	—10 CHARACTERS
UNITS OF MEASURE	—KILOMETER
SCALE FACTOR	—1000
NUMERIC TYPE	—INTEGER
NUMERIC PRECISION	—6 DIGITS
NUMERIC VALUE	—NEGATIVE
STORAGE FORMAT	—BINARY
RECORDING MODE	—FIXED
STORAGE LENGTH	—3 BYTES

- ACCESS AUTHORITY—a set of references to the organizational groups within the company who have the right to grant access to attribute values.
- AUTHORIZED USERS—a set of references to the organizational groups who have been granted access privileges to the information represented by the attribute and its physical representations. The references identify who uses the attribute and whether or not they can create, delete, or modify attribute values.
- VALUE-SET ASSIGNMENT RESPONSIBILITY—a set of references to the organizational groups who have the right to add to, delete from, or otherwise modify the set of acceptable values that can be assumed by the attribute values.
- ENTITY CLASS MEMBERSHIP—a reference to the ENTITY CLASS that includes the attribute as a component. The name must identify an entity class defined elsewhere in dictionary.
- LOGICAL GROUP MEMBERSHIP—a list of names identifying the LOGICAL GROUPS that include the attribute as a component. The names in the list must correspond to the names associated with logical group definitions recorded elsewhere in the dictionary.
- LOGICAL RECORD MEMBERSHIP—a list of names identifying the LOGICAL RECORDS containing physical representations of the attribute. The names included in the list must correspond to the names associated with logical record definitions recorded elsewhere in the dictionary.
- VALIDITY/EDIT RULES—a free-form narrative listing the edit rules that must be satisfied by attribute values stored in groups, segments, or similar physical data structures. The narrative includes, among other, syntactical rules dictating the format or internal structure of the attribute.
- CONSISTENCY CHECKS—a free-form narrative listing the consistency checks that must be satisfied by all attribute values. The narrative includes tables defining value correlations between related attributes.
- REASONABLENESS CHECKS—a narrative listing the reasonableness

checks which, when applied against attribute values, identify values which are reasonable and should be further investigated. The narrative includes tables identifying acceptable subsets of attribute values and the circumstances in which those restricted subsets apply.

- USAGE PROPAGATION—a free-form narrative describing the impact of changes made to attribute values held in physical data structures and the steps that must be taken to propagate the changes throughout the data base.
- VALIDATION PROPAGATION—a free-form narrative describing the impact of changes to the set of acceptable values that can be assumed by an attribute, and the action necessary to update the acceptable values of other related attributes. The narrative includes the names of attributes whose acceptable values can be affected by the changes.

8.7 CONTENTS OF A TYPICAL DATA DICTIONARY

The typical data dictionary's contents can be generally classified into three groups: data contents, processing contents, and environment contents.

Data contents describe or represent dictionary entries that are units of data; for example, attributes, entities, segments, and data bases.

Processing contents describe or represent dictionary entries that are processes, systems, programs, and transactions.

Environment contents describe or represent dictionary entries that are associated with the physical environment; for example, security features, users, terminals, and audit techniques.

8.7.1 The Data Dictionary as a Directory

"Data directory" is another term that is frequently used. As a rule, a dictionary gives the descriptions and definitions of an organization's data, whereas the directory gives the storage location of that data. However, many software vendors use these terms interchangeably, although some consistently use one or the other.

A data dictionary may contain a lot more than the location of stored data. It may be considered to be a machine-readable definition of a computerized data base. It is often used by a Data Base Management System to obtain the sizes, formats, and locations of data records and fields. A data dictionary may be considered a superset that can contain additional data and definitions. Some vendors of Data Base Management Systems now use the term "catalog" instead of "directory" or "dictionary." This usually means that the system includes a repository of metadata that is more extensive than the usual directory, but not as elaborate as a dictionary.

8.8 MAINTENANCE OF THE DATA DICTIONARY

The most important reason for the existence of a data dictionary is its ability to produce reports that are accurate and timely. For this reason, the maintenance of an organization's data dictionary is a very critical issue.

The maintenance of the data dictionary should be carried out in the following areas:

- the definitive information (the definition of entries)
- propagation effects and control of changes
- access authorization of users
- consistency/validation checks
- directory/data storage features
- relationship/membership of entry
- environmental data

The definitive information of the data dictionary will include the naming convention, the description and function of the entry, who is responsible for the definition and any subsequent update, and the data representation of the definition. Any maintenance carried out on the entries will ensure that the definitive information is correct and always reflects the current status in both accuracy and timeliness.

Any changes to the data dictionary contents should be made only after the effect of that change is evaluated. The person responsible for changes should determine which users, which programs and systems, and which relationships/cross-references will be affected. Ideally, all changes should be done from one central terminal or controlled by one central organization. Unauthorized or unapproved changes should never be allowed in the dictionary environment.

8.8.1 Access Authorization of Users

The data dictionary should always contain accurate and timely information on the access authorization of all users. This information should not only include access to the data dictionary itself, but also to the stored data. Any change in access authorization of a user should be immediately shown in the dictionary and appropriate measures taken to maintain the existing data-security level.

8.8.2 Consistency/Validation Checks

Because of the multi-origin of names and definitions in the data dictionary, the number of inconsistencies in names is often very high. Some organizations attempt to cut down on these cases by having several versions of the project data dictionary, and one dictionary designated as the corporate dictionary. Names and definitions are migrated to the corporate dictionary only when it is established that no changes will be made to the entry. For this reason, the need for maintenance of the corporate dictionary seldom arises.

8.8.3 Directory/Data Storage Features

One function of the data dictionary is to act as a directory or pointer to the stored data or to the metadata. The dictionary may contain unique identifiers which will allow the user to determine the location of the metadata formats. For example, in a particular data dictionary developed in-house, the metadata was stored on seven volumes of disk storage. Each category of the definition carried an entry called "Library Identifier." This identifier took the form 'XXXNNNNN,' where 'XXX' was a three-character alphabetic field identifying the volume containing the definition, and 'NNNNN' was a five-character numeric field which served as a unique identifier within a volume.

A user wishing to access the dictionary definitions need only code the Library Identifier in the Job Control Language (JCL) if running a batch mode, or enter the identifier when required to do so, if running in an interactive mode.

8.8.4 Relationship/Membership of Entry

A very important feature of the data dictionary is its ability to show relationships between an attribute and the record to which it belongs, a file and its data base, and a data base and its logical schema. It is very important that these relationships are properly maintained. During update or deletion activities, these linkages must be maintained.

8.8.5 Environmental Data

Many data dictionaries contain entries describing the operating environment of the organization. For example, the entries may indicate whether a traditional operating environment or a data base environment is used.

Other dictionaries may indicate the storage media for stored data or metadata. The maintenance aspect of data dictionaries must account for any change in the operating environment.

8.9 ACTIVE AND PASSIVE DICTIONARIES

Dictionaries are generally classified into two categories: *active* and *passive*.

In the passive mode, the dictionary is used mainly as a repository of information on attributes, records, files, data bases, and schemas. A user wanting access to this information may go to a shelf and retrieve this information from the dictionary, or retrieve it from a computer, if the dictionary is computerized.

In the active mode, the dictionary may be used in conjunction with the operating system to lock out unauthorized users from stored data or metadata. For example, the dictionary may contain an authorization table showing the names of users and the data they are authorized to access. A request from a user is channeled to the data dictionary and access authorization determined. If the request is legitimate, access to the data is granted. If the request exceeds the authorization, the request is denied and an audit trail for an *ex post facto* analysis is created.

In an active mode, the data dictionary can be used for the automated design of data bases. The feature is very often difficult to implement, and may still be several years in the future for most organizations.

8.10 DESIGN OF DATA DICTIONARIES

The next chapter will discuss in detail the design of data dictionaries. This section will serve to introduce the design of a basic data dictionary.

Data dictionaries are designed to give definite information about objects in which an organization may have an interest. The entries in the dictionary may include: attributes, entities, records, files, and databases.

The typical entries for an attribute will include, among others, the name, any aliases, the description and function, data length, origin of definition of attribute, validity, update authorization, security, and consistency checks.

In addition to the above, the design should include features for accessing and retrieving from the dictionary.

8.11 CONTROL AND AUDIT FEATURES OF THE DATA DICTIONARY

The data dictionary can be used as a tool to control access to an organization's data. It can also be used by internal auditors to monitor the data-security efforts of an organization.

In the area of controls, the data dictionary can be used to control changes to attributes, entities, or files. By including the names of those responsible for making changes in the dictionary, the organization can limit this activity to authorized individuals.

The dictionary can also be used to control the effects that changes would have on users, programs, and applications. By including the names of those affected by changes, the organization can immediately notify those affected.

The dictionary can be used in both the active and passive modes to control access, not only to metadata, but also to the stored data. An access-authorization table contained in the dictionary can be used to control access to data.

Internal auditors can use the data dictionary during systems development to ensure that agreed-upon standards are being adhered to by systems designers. They can use it to audit naming conventions and standards, to determine who authorized users of the system are and their authorization levels.

The data dictionary can be used in an active mode to interface with the operating system to produce audit trails to analyze attempts made by users to breach the organization's security.

8.12 DATA DICTIONARY STANDARDS

Data dictionary standards may fall into any of the following categories:

- metadata contents
- interface to external environment
- interface with command languages
- access rules and control
- customized and management reports
- security
- interrelations between entries
- extensibility

Standards in metadata contents would clearly indicate which entries should be found in the dictionary. For example, the standard entry for an attribute should include: name, function, description, alias, definition responsibility, standard representation, edit rules, and access control features.

A dictionary design should include standards for interfacing with the external environment. In this regard, the standards may be as simple as including an entry describing the physical environment and its operating system, or as difficult as using the data dictionary to control access to the stored data and the operating system itself.

Standards for interfacing with command languages would indicate how high-level languages, such as Fortran and PL1, will use the data dictionary to build file structures and layouts, and how retrievel languages will access the data dictionary itself.

Standards for access rules and control would indicate who can access the dictionary, how the dictionary contents would be accessed, whether the contents would be accessed in its original form, or whether copies of the data would be accessed.

Standards in the area of security would cover the security of the data dictionary and its contents, and security techniques for protecting the external environment.

Standards indicating the interrelations among entries would show how an attribute is related to a group, record, file, or data base. In the reverse order, the standards should show what attributes comprise the data base, entity, or file.

Standards in the area of extensibility would indicate what features can be included by the users and how the user can enhance the dictionary capability or make it more user-friendly.

8.13 THE ANSI X3/H4 COMMITTEE ON DATA DICTIONARY STANDARDS

Since 1983, I have been a member of the ANSI X3/H4 Committee on data dictionary standards. This committee has been empowered by the International Standards Organization and the National Bureau of Standards to develop a standard for manufacturers of data dictionaries. Although the emphasis is placed on manufacturers who intend to supply the United States government, it is hoped that other manufacturers will comply with the standards.

The committee's efforts are centered around naming conventions, the interfaces to the dictionary, and the entity-relationship model that will represent the data base.

It is interesting to note that several members of the committee who fully support the Information Resource Dictionary System (IRDS) are engaged in developing standards or dictionaries for their own organizations. For example, IBM is developing the Repository, and other CASE tool vendors are developing their own dictionaries. It is my hope that, if IRDS becomes the standard, then other dictionary vendors will build interfaces to IRDS or make it relatively easy to import/export data across dictionaries.

It is not my intention to discuss the volumes of documents that have come out of the X3/H4 committee over the years. It will suffice to state that these documents are now widely available from the American National Standards Institute (ANSI).

8.14 THE DATA DICTIONARY AS A TOOL FOR DATA ANALYSIS

Data Analysis is defined as documenting the entities in which the organization has an interest. It is in this area that the data dictionary is most useful. In data analysis, the organization attempts to determine the entities and the role they play. The data dictionary can be used to record this information. The dictionary would give not only definitive information about the entities, but also the relationships between the entities and how these entities can be used to model the organization's data environment.

During data analysis, inconsistencies, redundancies, and incompleteness in the data are determined. A source for such determinations is the data dictionary.

Again, the development teams may want to determine the originators of the definition during data analysis, whether the definition has homonyms or synonyms, and the aliases by which the definition may be identified. The dictionary should be the supplier of information to satisfy these queries.

Finally, the entries (metadata) in the data dictionary serve as a useful guideline or standard that can be followed by the data analyst who wishes to document information about attributes, entities, and relationships in an efficient and structured manner.

9

The Data Dictionary in Systems Design

9.1 INTRODUCTION

The role of the data dictionary in the design, implementation, and maintenance of data base systems has been well documented in the current literature.

The growing awareness of data as a corporate resource, resulting in data-driven, rather then process-driven, systems has led to a recognition of the impact of data on departments outside of data processing. In this way, the systems development life cycle has developed away from a point where the focus of concern was on highly localized data processing problems. It is now recognized that the efficiency of a given system usually depends upon its end-user orientation and how well it represents and serves the organization as a whole. Current methodologies are becoming less process-oriented and more data-oriented.

It is because of this new awareness that the data dictionary can play a significant part in supporting the SDLC. It provides a wealth of detail on which early research work can be based, and is then an invaluable communications tool between the different departments that are involved in the SDLC.

It is for these reasons that the succeeding sections discuss the role of the data dictionary in the SDLC.

9.2 WHAT IS A DATA DICTIONARY?

A data dictionary can be defined as an organized reference to the data content of an organization's programs, systems, data bases, collections of all files, or manual records.

The data dictionary may be maintained manually or by computer. The term data dictionary sometimes specifically refers to a software product that is utilized to maintain a dictionary data base. The data dictionary will contain names, descriptions, and definitions of the organization's data resources.

9.3 THE CONCEPT OF METADATA

In the broadest sense, a data dictionary is *any* organized collection of information about data.

In the real world, any information system, whether or not it is computerized, exists to store and process data about objects (entities). Data records can then be created to represent occurrences of these entities. We define specific record types to represent specific entity types. Frequently, we also assign keys or identifiers, such as customer names and invoice numbers, to differentiate one record occurrence from another. A data dictionary can then be designed that contains data about those customer and invoice record types.

The customer and invoice records in the data base contain ordinary data. The record in the data dictionary contains metadata, or data about the data. For example, the record in the data dictionary may contain the name, the record length, the data characteristics, and the recording mode of the record in the data base.

9.4 ACTIVE VERSUS PASSIVE DATA DICTIONARIES

Data dictionaries are often categorized as active or passive. This refers to the extent of their integration with the data base management system. If the data dictionary and the DBMS are integrated to the extent that the DBMS uses the definitions in the dictionary at run time, the dictionary is active. If the dictionary is freestanding or independent of the DBMS, it is passive.

An active dictionary must contain an accurate, up-to-date description of the physical data base in order for the data base management system to access the data.

In a passive dictionary environment, more effort is required to keep two copies of the same data, and great care must be taken to ensure that the two copies are actually identical.

9.5 THE ROLE OF THE DATA DICTIONARY IN THE SDLC

The role of the data dictionary in the Systems Development Life Cycle (SDLC) is best exemplified in Figure 9.1.

Any analysis of Figure 9.1 will show that the data dictionary is at the core of

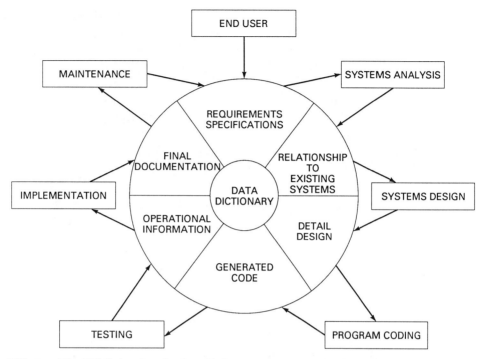

FIG. 9.1. The SDLC showing the data dictionary as a communication and documentation tool.

systems design and development. The metadata collected in the dictionary about the different phases of the SDLC are demonstrated in the second layer of the diagram. The third layer depicts the various interfaces to the different phases of the SDLC. The directions of the arrows indicate that the interfaces act as input to the phases and also extract design information from the phases.

As we move in a clockwise direction around the second layer, we notice, starting with the input from the end users, that the following types of metadata are collected:

- Requirements specifications
- Relationships to existing systems
- Detail design
- Generated code
- Operational information
- Final documentation

9.5.1 Requirements Specifications

As indicated in Chapter 2, the systems analyst or the data analyst collects data from the end user on the entities in which there is a particular interest. Definitions and descriptions about the entities, data characteristics, security requirements, attribute content, and processes involved in moving the data across interfaces may be collected, as well as manipulating that data.

The analyst synthesizes this data and then enters as much of it into the data dictionary as the constructs of the dictionary allow. For example, in the DATAMA-NAGER data dictionary marketed by Manager Software Products (MSP), the analyst can enter data about the system, file, groups of data, and data items that will constitute a solution to the user's requirements.

9.5.2 Relationships to Existing Systems

In arriving at what may be the optimum solution to the user's requirements, the analyst must seek to determine from the dictionary whether:

- A system already exists that can solve the problem.
- If no system exists, what portions of the existing systems can be used in the solution.
- Alternate solutions can be obtained.

9.5.3 Detail Design

During detail system design, the analyst will enter data about the data models, the process flows, the programming specifications, the file layouts, and report formats. If the current design has any relationship to designs already existing in the data dictionary, the analyst can extract that portion and implement it with the new metadata.

9.5.4 Generated Code

The data dictionary contains copy books (source statements) and source statements, or pointers to source statement libraries, which may be extracted to use for program testing.

It is now possible to generate code from process definitions and programming specifications stored in the data dictionary. Current CASE tools can generate this code for several languages and several different platforms, e.g., PCs or mainframes.

9.5.5 Operational Information

The data dictionary may contain information that will enable the data processing staff to execute the programs. This information may include run instructions, job control language (JCL) set up, distribution information, test plans and requirements, and processing exceptions.

9.5.6 Final Documentation

The final documentation information stored in the data dictionary may include user-manual instructions, impact analysis information, acceptance testing and sign-off information, change control information, and JCL information.

9.6 INTERFACES TO THE DATA DICTIONARY

Interfaces to the data dictionary are many and varied. They act in two directions: as output to the dictionary, and as extracts from the dictionary. These interfaces include:

- End User
- Systems Analysis
- Systems Design
- Program Coding
- Testing
- Implementation
- Maintenance

9.6.1 The End User

The end user is the primary source of input during the requirements specifications phase of systems development. It is during this phase that data is collected on the objectives and scope of the project, the data and processing requirements, the operating environment, alternative processing, data security, and the input and output formats.

The advent of data base management systems, structured design methodologies, and new development tools has signalled a larger role for the end user in systems development. The end user is as much a part of the systems development team as the data analyst or systems analyst. The success or failure of the system depends, to a large degree, on the quality of the data collected from user requirements.

9.6.2 The Systems Analysis Phase

During the systems analysis phase, data is obtained from the end user and the user requirements specifications, fed into the systems design phase, and the relationship to existing systems data is stored in the data dictionary.

During this phase, the data and systems analysts will iteratively extract data from the requirements specifications already stored in the data dictionary, augment it with that from the end user and any obtained from existing systems, and come up with data and process models that form the primary output of the systems design phase.

If, during the systems analysis phase, no data is found in the data dictionary that connects the current system with other systems, the analyst enters any existing relationships into the data dictionary.

9.6.3 The Systems Design Phase

During the systems design phase, the data analyst extracts information from the analysis phase and relationships to existing systems stored in the data dictionary and develops a data model. This model is, in turn, stored in the data dictionary as detail design metadata. Meanwhile, the systems (process) analyst develops a process model with information from the data dictionary and the systems analysis phase. The data collected during this phase is stored in the detail design section of the data dictionary and used as input, through programming specifications, to the program coding phase.

9.6.4 The Program Coding Phase

During the program coding phase, the programmer/analyst takes the specifications from the systems design phase and couples them with metadata from the detail design information stored in the data dictionary to produce program code for the testing phase and to store the information as metadata, and sometimes as source data, in the data dictionary.

9.6.5 The Testing Phase

During this phase, the analysts take program code from the program coding phase and the generated code stored in the data dictionary and test them to obtain operational metadata to be stored in the data dictionary and program code for the implementation phase.

9.6.6 The Implementation Phase

During this phase, operational information metadata stored in the data dictionary is coupled with the tested program code to produce implementable systems. The resulting data from this phase are stored in the data dictionary as a final document, and are used as input data for the maintenance phase.

9.6.7 The Maintenance Phase

During this phase, metadata from the final document stored in the data dictionary and retrieved from the implementation phase are used to maintain the production systems.

This phase also encompasses the updating of requirements specifications stored in the data dictionary and constant reporting of the results of these changes are available to the user.

9.7 THE DATA DICTIONARY AS A DOCUMENTATION TOOL

As has been mentioned earlier the data dictionary plays significant roles in the systems development life cycle. One major role is that of documenting the results of each phase of the SDLC. This section describes some of the entries that are documented in the data dictionary for the major phases of the SDLC.

9.7.1 Documenting the System Design Phase

The data dictionary can offer substantial assistance to the designer during the system design phase, by acting as the source and storage of the inputs and outputs of the design step.

The inputs to data design are full descriptions of the business processes and of the data required by these processes. The outputs are the logical views and the logical data base (also known as logical schemas). A logical data base refers to a structuring of entities, and relations between entities, supporting the business processes of the application.

There are many different methods of transforming the business processes and their required data into a logical data base. One is a top-down data design method identifying entities and the relationships between the entities before defining the attributes of each entity.

Alternatively, there are bottom-up data design techniques, which encourage the description of entities, and the attributes identifying the entities, before identifying the relationships between entities.

There are five basic steps in top-down data design:

- Identifying the business functions of the application.
- Identifying the data required by each function and the procedure by which data is collected.
- Identifying the entities of the application.
- Defining the relationships between the entities.
- Ascribing attributes to their entities.

Nowhere is the importance of the data dictionary more obvious than it is in the building of the function's logical model. As the keeper of the *who, what,* and *how* of the organizational information system, the data dictionary provides full descriptions of:

- The business functions
- The data generated and used by the business functions
- The application entities
- The relationships of the application's entities to one another
- The attributes of the entities

Frequently, data itself goes through an evolutionary process, its definition becoming more and more refined until it can finally be set. Data can also be perceived simultaneously from several user points of view. A data dictionary that has facilities for multiple logical dictionaries can document the history of a data item or process as well as hold these varied points of view. This can be a most valuable aid during the design stage.

9.7.2 Documenting the Detailed Design Phase

In a Business System Plan (BSP), the design phase is comprised of two levels, the General Design and the Detailed Design, in which business activities, data, entities, relationships, and attributes are described, not just on the applications level, but from a higher level providing a corporate, transfunctional perspective. In BSP, the methodology is the same as with SDLC; it is simply engineered on a higher plane. Once these elements are plugged in, they remain in documented form on the data dictionary and can also be accessed for future systems development. Another feature of the data dictionary that can prove to be most useful at this point in the SDLC is its facility for providing implicit, as well as explicit relationships. The systems designer, who might otherwise overlook these implicit relationships, is spared one more trap that might otherwise be fallen into.

9.7.3 Documenting the Physical Design Phase

The details of physical design depend very much on the characteristics of the DBMS chosen for the data base design.

In an IMS environment, the physical design includes the following selections:

- Physical data bases and types of logical relationships, whether unidirectionally or bidirectionally physically paired.
- Access methods, whether HISAM, HIDAM, or HDAM.
- Segments, hierarchical structures, and data representation, including type and size.

- Secondary indices.
- Types of pointers in relationships.

The data dictionary is a very useful tool to document these selections. In addition, volume and usage statistics necessary for the ordering of data base segments and for the determination of storage estimates can be documented in the data dictionary.

9.7.4 Documenting the Implementation Phase

The implementation phase is very often not considered a part of the SDLC because, by that point, the system has been installed and consequently has entered a separate, operational period.

It is a stage that has enormous impact, not just on the system, but on the entire organization as well. Maintenance is also a task that is especially well served by the data dictionary, which can provide:

- Complete up-to-date documentation of the system.
- An historical and multiuser perspective view of the development of the definitions of the systems entities, process entities, and the relationships among them.
- Enforcement of the use of definitions in a logical manner.
- Security of the integrity of these definitions.
- The means of assessing the impact of system changes.

Consequently, the maintenance staff is provided with a comprehensive and logically consistent picture of the system, it's functions, processes, and data components. They are thus properly prepared to respond to changes in the means by which error is minimized and time, money, and frustration saved.

The maintenance stage is also the point at which the use of the data dictionary as a systems development tool is most easily validated. Systems founded upon data dictionary resources are the most likely to be spared the unnecessary and yet most typical function of maintenance, namely rectification of bad systems planning and specifications. Consequently, these types are the ones most likely to free the maintenance stage for its proper function of adapting the system to the organization's changing environment. Obviously, this frees the staff for the development of new systems and reduces many of the external pressures otherwise imposed on all systems.

9.7.5 Documenting the Structured Maintenance Phase

Structured maintenance deals with the procedures and guidelines used to achieve system change or evolution through the definition of data structure change in order to accommodate the requirements of system change. The inputs to structured maintenance are user change requests and the current system, including data base design and systems design. These are included in the data dictionary. The output from structured maintenance is, ideally, a system reflecting the user change request.

There are five steps to structured maintenance:

- The identification of the changes to the data structures required to accommodate the user request.
- The identification of the program functions that currently process the data structures. These program functions are reviewed and systems changes are identified.
- The determination of the cost of the change. One of the benefits of this method is that it quickly indicates significant costly changes, seen when the data structures required to accommodate the change are very different from the current data structures.
- Performance of the implementation—if the cost is acceptable.
- Testing of the results.

Structured maintenance thus goes through all of the steps of the structured system development methodology, as defined here.

This is an effective way to minimize the need to have to recover from past mistakes of the system, whether they are the result of unstructured or structured methodologies.

A system development life cycle is used to produce the means by which the organizational data is to be manipulated. Before it may be manipulated, however, it must be managed, and that is the function of the data dictionary.

9.8 THE DATA DICTIONARY AND DATA SECURITY

The data dictionary can be used in the data base environment, to protect the organization's data. Entries may be used to indicate who has access rights to what data and who can update or alter that data. It can also be used to indicate who has responsibility for creating and changing definitions.

Current data dictionaries utilize several different protection mechanisms to effect data security. in an Data dictionaries can also have pointers, in an AUTHORIZATION section, to various data security software packages. Some of these are:

- Access management
- Privacy transformations
- Cryptographic controls
- Security kernels
- Access matrix

Due to space constraints, it is not possible to discuss all of the mechanisms at length. The reader will, instead, be referred to some of the current literature on data security. A brief discussion on some of them, however, is given in the following paragraphs.

9.8.1 Access Management

These techniques are aimed at preventing unauthorized users from obtaining services from the system or gaining access to its files. The procedures involved are authorization, identification, and authentication. Authorization is given for certain users to enter the data base and request certain types of information. Users attempting to enter the system must first identify themselves and their locations, and then authenticate the identification.

9.8.2 Privacy Transformations

Privacy transformations are techniques for concealing information by coding the data in user-precessor communications or in files. Privacy transformations consist of sets of logical operations on the individual characters of the data. Privacy transformations break down into two general types—irreversible and reversible. Irreversible privacy transformations include aggregation and random modification. In this case, valid statistics can be obtained from such data, but individual values cannot be obtained.

Reversible privacy transformations are comprised of the following types:

- Coding— Replacement of a group of words in one language by a word in another language.

- Compression— Removal of redundancies and blanks from transmitted data.

- Substitution— Replacement of letters in one or more items.

- Transposition— Distortion of the sequence of letters in the ciphered text; all letters in the original text are retained in this technique.

- Composite Transformation— Combinations of the above methods.

9.8.3 Cryptographic Controls

Cryptographic transformations were recognized long ago as an effective protection mechanism in communication systems. In the past, they were used mainly to protect information transferred through communication lines.

There is still much debate about the cost/benefit ratio of encrypting large data bases. The author's experiences with encryption indicate that the cost of producing clear text from large encrypted data bases is prohibitive.

9.8.4 Security Kernels

Security kernels, as the name suggests, are extra layers of protection surrounding operating systems. The kernels are usually software programs that are used to test for authenticity, and to either authorize or deny all user requests to the operating system.

A request to the operating system to execute a task or retrieve data from the data base is routed to the security kernel, where the request is examined to determine whether the user is authorized to access the requested data. If all checks are passed, the request is transmitted to the operating system, which then executes the request.

9.9 DATA DICTIONARY STANDARDS

There are two types of data-related standards for data dictionaries: data definition standards and data format conformance.

Data definition refers to a standard way of describing data. One example is the naming of data. The naming standard may be in the form of rigid rules or established conventions for assigning names to data entities. All user areas within the enterprise will know that, for instance, the data element "customer name"—used in files, programs, and reports—means the same throughout the enterprise.

Data format conformance is content-related. It means that a data element, in addition to having the same name throughout the enterprise, also must conform to a common set of format rules for the data element to retain the same meaning. For example, all data elements involving "data" should have the same format throughout the enterprise—and only that format should be assigned. Similarly, if codes are to be used throughout the enterprise, these must be uniform. If an acceptable state code is two-letters, that must be the universally accepted code in the enterprise, and no other code, whether one-, three-, or four-letters, should be used.

9.9.1 Standard Formats for Data Dictionary Entries

Standards are required for the format and content used in defining and describing meta-entities of the data dictionary. This means setting standards for the type of information that must be collected for each entry type and, most importantly, for the conventions that must be observed in defining these attributes. In effect, this amounts to defining a set of standards for methods of preparing attribute, entity, and relationship descriptions.

There are a number of general guidelines for establishing a standard. Several standard entries are available in commercially produced dictionaries. However, a

TABLE 9.1. Sample Standard for Data Element Description.

Data Element	Definition
Identification Number	A 7-character unique identifier beginning with ELXXXXX.
Designator	A short name composed of the keywords of the DESCRIPTION.
Programming Name	An abbreviated form of the DESIGNATOR using only approved abbreviations. *Example:* LEGL-CUST-NAME.
Description	A narrative explanation of the data element; the first sentence must indentify the real-world entity being described. The second sentence may expand on usage characteristics. *Example:* The name of a customer, which is the legal name. It may not be the commonly used name. It is usually derived from legal papers.

typical standard entry for a data element is illustrated in Table 9.1. A data element may be described in terms of the attributes in this figure.

9.9.2 Standards for Programs Interfacing with a Data Dictionary

Data dictionary standards for programming interfaces basically fall into the area of the structure of the "call" statement from the programming language to the dictionary package.

Other standards in this area will indicate how high-level languages will use the data dictionary to build file structures and record layouts from "COPY" books. They will also indicate how these languages will access the dictionary itself.

9.9.3 Security Standards

Standards for access rules and controls will indicate who can access the dictionary, how the dictionary will be accessed, and whether the contents will be accessed in their original form or as copies.

Standards in the area of security will cover the use of the data dictionary as a protection mechanism and the entries that must be made in the data dictionary to achieve those standards.

9.10 EXAMPLES OF DATA DICTIONARY ENTRIES

There are several commercially available data dictionaries, each with its own meta-data entries and standards. This section illustrates entries for three available dictionaries:

- IBM DB/DC
- MSP Datamanager
- Xerox Data Dictionary (XDD)

9.10.1 The Xerox Data Dictionary

Functional requirements. The dictionary software must process certain essential features to properly support the Xerox administrative and data processing environment including:

- Local users and data administrators, in controlling their data processing environment.
- Multinational systems designers and users.
- Technical designers and programmers, in implementing and maintaining systems on a local and multinational level.
- Audit, security, and systems control needs of Xerox management.

These functions can be divided into twelve categories:

1. Data Definitions, used to:

   - Describe data elements.
   - Describe physical and logical records.
   - Allow for the mechanical generation of an entity code or name.
   - Relate elements and records to programs and modules.

2. Data Administration:

   - Supports data element definition.
   - Describes the usage of standards and procedures in programs, systems, and data entries.
   - Relates entity definitions to authorized owners.
   - Renames dictionary entities.

3. System and Program Definition and Support, used to:

   - Describe programs.
   - Provide for the description of functional interfaces.
   - Relate a program or module to other programs or modules that call and are called by the program or module.
   - Describe and generate on-line screen formatting characteristics.

4. User Access, allowing:

   - The cross-referencing of all dictionary defined entities.
   - Access to any dictionary defined entity by its generic name, entity code, or *Alias.*
   - "Where used" reporting for all entities single and full level.
   - COPY and MACRO library member generation.
   - On-line access for inquiry and update.

5. Data base Definition Administration, used to:

   - Describe data bases (one definition per database).
   - Relate data bases to their components and to programs.
   - Relate data bases to elements.
   - Mechanically generate data definitions and relationships for data base development (e.g., DBDs, PSBs, etc.).
   - Provide interface for external entity editing control for dictionary transactions.

6. The Data Dictionary:

   - All organizations involved in data definitions and usage will maintain records describing the data entities and usage and their relationships.
   - Corporate data-naming standards and attribute definitions will be followed for all mechanized data dictionaries.
   - All information systems' organizations should establish migration strategies to the Xerox Data Dictionary for all operational systems.

7. Data Element Attributes:

   - Element Name—specifies the descriptive name of the data element.
   - Element Description—provides narrative text/description of the data element.
   - Element Length—specifies the number of positions required for one occurrence of the data element as entered.
   - Element Format—specifies the character category of the element, such as numeric or alphabetic.
   - Responsibility—specifies the organization or function responsible for the data element definition.

8. Security types:

- Registered.
- Private.
- Unclassified.
- Personal.

9. Specification Status:

- Draft—applies to data entered into the dictionary for the purpose of facilitating the early portion of the systems design process.
- Proposed—A user using the dictionary proposes an addition, deletion, or change to meet a system's requirement.
- Approved—When testing is completed to the satisfaction of the administrator, the specification's status is changed to "approved."
- Active—This indicates that the entity is being used in a production system.

10. Synonym:
    1. This specifies a data element as having nearly the same name and/or meaning as another element.
11. Coding/Edit Rules:
    1. This indicates coding structures, conventions, composition, and any special edit rules.
12. Data Dictionary Naming Standards:

- Primary Name—Primary names for elements and groups will be descriptive English, not exceeding 32 characters.
- Higher Level Entities—No classword is required on items or groups, but for higher level entities, a leading classword is to be used, such as SYS-XXXX.

9.10.2 MSP Datamanager

The MSP Datamanager is a data dictionary marketed by Manager Software Products (MSP). It has the following basic structure:

- System
- Program
- Module
- File
- Group
- Data Item

The data structure is useful to both the user and the data dictionary in terms of establishing data relationships and the levels of importance of each of the above member types.

9.10.3 A Discussion of Member Types

System. This is the highest level of the member-type hierarchy. These can be subsystems to other systems. These can be declarations of the programs, modules, files, groups, and data items processed in the system.

Program. This member contains or calls other programs and/or modules; and inputs, outputs, or updates files, groups, and/or data items.

Module. This is an independent set of instructions, which may be used by other programs.

File. This member may be manual or automated. It contains records, which contain groups and/or data items. It may also contain other files.

Group. This is a combination of data items and/or other groups. It may be an entire record or a subset of data items found on a record. It may be used to describe information on a preprinted form.

Data item. This is the fundamental element of data. Smallest name unit into which data is divided in the user organization.

9.10.4 Entries in Datamanager

```
Prepared By: Freida Jones    'Year in Production-1988'
System
Effective Date               '10-9-85'
Obsolete Date                '12-31-99'
Alias                        'MGA'
Contains
                             'MGA03001-XTRACT-IPMF'
                             'MGA03002-CREATE-IPMF'
                             'MGA03003-SELECT-IPMF'
                             'MGA03003-CREATE-UPD'
                             'MGA03004-TAG-PURGED'
Frequency Run                'Weekly'
Catalog                      'System'
                             'batch'
Catalog-owner                'Annette Smith'
Note                         'Year in Production-1988'
Administrative-Data          'Application Narrative'
Project ID:                  'Project ID. MGAP'
Prepared By: Freida Jones          Date: 10_19_88
```

A. System Objective:
   To function as an interface between Cycare-based Medical Group systems and the new IPMF update processing system.

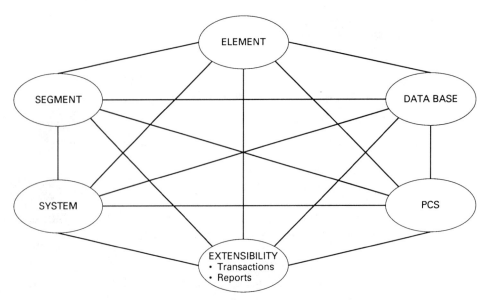

FIG. 9.2. Dictionary data bases.

  B. System Functions:
    1. To reformat IPMF and transmittal tapes for subsequent processing.
    2. To generate a summary of all changes made to a particular policy.
    3. To provide a copy of all updating transmittals to all Cycare-based Medical
       Centers, properly flagged according to changes undergone by each policy.
  C. System Features:
    MGA uses inputs from the registration and capitation systems.

9.10.5 The IBM DB/DC Data Dictionary

The DB/DC data dictionary is comprised of a set of data bases that are used to store and access information about an installation's data processing resources.
    The dictionary contains information about data (see Figure 9.2).

Subject Categories.

  ▪ IBM defined:
    Systems/Subsystems
    Jobs
    Programs/modules
    Data bases
    PSBs/PCBs
    Segments/records
    Data elements (see Figure 9.3.)

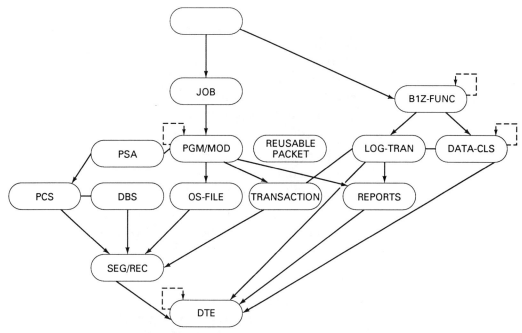

FIG. 9.3. Data dictionary relationship diagram.

- Installation defined
    Business function
    Logical transactions
    Data classes
    Physical transactions
    Reports
    OS files
    Reusable packets

Information on Subjects.

- Name
    Unique/meaningful
    Primary/alias
    1 to 31 positions/language (BAL/Cobol/PL/I)

- Attributes dependent on:
    Category
    Language of program
    Length of a data element

- Description:
    Descriptive name (user name) on line one
    Any descriptive matter starts on line three
    999 lines total, of 72 positions each

- User data:
  - Provision for five separate types
  - Audit trail
  - Edit criteria
  - System identification
  - Reusable packet information
  - Application-related information

- Relationships:
  - To other entities
  - Of the system to a job
  - Of the job to a program

- Relationship data:
  - Information about the relationship between two entities
  - Indicative key (data element within segment)

Identification of subjects (dictionary name)

- Components of a name
  - Status code, which identifies the status of an entity
  - Subject category (code), which identifies the subject category
  - Name, which is the primary name on the dictionary
  - Occurrences, which Distinguishes between different physical attributes

- All of the identifiers are required while working with a subject (Subject name)

Accessing the dictionary

- Interactive on-line facility
  - Screens for each subject
  - Prompts for user actions
  - Screen to screen access (menu to menu access)
  - Available through TSO terminals
  - Used for entry/update/retrieval

- Batch forms
  - Card image
  - Identifying control information on each record
  - Bulk data processing
  - For entering only
  - Available through TSO

- Commands
  - Interactive on-line
  - Within batch processing
  - Example: scan, change name, report

TABLE 9.2. Entry of Information into the Data Dictionary.

Project Life Cycle	Data Base Design	Data Dictionary Documentation
Feasibility	Conceptual design	System/subsystems Business functions Data classes
Functional analysis	Detailed conceptual design	Logical transactions data Elements reports
System design	Logical data base design	Segments Jobs Program/modules Reusable packets OS files Physical transactions
Implementation	Physical data base design	Data bases PSBs (Program Specification Blocks)/PCBs (Program Control Blocks)

Procedure for documentation.

- Applications group fills out data dictionary input forms
- Data dictionary group reviews and enters data
- Data dictionary group runs reports and delivers them to the applications group
- Input forms may also be used for corrections
- Order of entities follows the order of the PLC

Data element entry procedure.

- Applications project team
   Identifies and describes data elements by user name

- Supplies data element I/P forms to the data dictionary administration (see Table 9.2)
- Data dictionary administration
   Assigns descriptors
   Performs redundancy analysis
   Develops Cobol names
   Assigns BAL name
   Enters data elements in dictionary
   Sends data elements and cross reference report to application project team

9.11 SUMMARY

This chapter discussed the role of the data dictionary in the development of systems in a data base environment. It indicated what inputs and outputs the dictionary generated for each phase and their interface with the relevant phase personnel.

The chapter closed with a summary of the structure of three data dictionaries. The last two are very successful and widely used.

Readers are referred to the detailed coverage of data dictionaries discussed in the author's book *Analysis, Design, and Implementation of Data Dictionaries,* published in 1988 by McGraw-Hill.

10

Systems Design Using CASE Tools

10.1 INTRODUCTORY REMARKS

Computer-aided software engineering (CASE) has been promoted as the panacea for curing an organization's backlog problems in meeting development schedules, coordinating design efforts, and maintaining its systems. It has also been touted as the tool to increase programmer and systems designer productivity, as much as two to ten times.

This chapter will introduce CASE tools as a design and development aid. It will discuss some selection criteria for deciding on the tool that will best suit a particular environment. Finally, it will list some vendors of CASE tools and the contacts within each vendor.

10.2 SEVERAL DEFINITIONS OF CASE

CASE, although now widely accepted as an acronym, does not yet have a single, widely accepted definition. Perhaps a more appropriate acronym would be CASD (computer-aided systems development), which could be defined as "computers applied to aid in any aspect of systems development."

Because CASE can encompass so many aspects of systems development, the question "When is CASE the right choice?" must be addressed separately for each of three types of CASE tools:

1. Programmer/Project Productivity Tools—Provides support for the designers and programmers of software, but only at the back end of the systems development life cycle. These may include tools for natural language programming, project management, and documentation.

2. Systems Development Methodology Tools—Most systems development methodologies are collections of techniques, combined in structures made up to minimize redundant effort and maximize coordination between tasks. These methodology tools provide support for and enforce a systems development methodology at any or all stages of the life cycle. They may include any of the systems development support tools as appropriate for the methodology. In addition, they enforce methodology rules and thus provide systems development expertise to the users.

3. Systems Development Support Tools—These tools provide support for techniques and tasks of systems development at any or all stages of the life cycle, but do not necessarily enforce a systems development methodology. These may include diagramming tools, data dictionaries and analysis tools, or any of the productivity tools. (See Figure 10.1 for a diagram produced by a diagramming tool.)

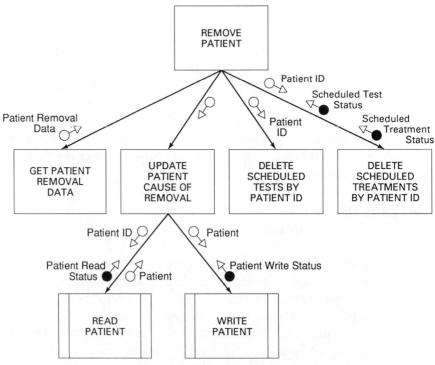

FIG. 10.1. Yourdon structure chart.

10.3 CATEGORIES OF
CASE TOOLS

An individual CASE tool automates one small, focused step in the life-cycle process. Individual tools fall into these general categories:

- Diagramming tools for pictorially representing system specifications.
- Screen and report painters for creating system specifications and for simple prototyping.
- Dictionaries, information management systems, and facilities to store, report, and query technical and project-management system information.
- Specification—checking tools to detect incomplete, syntactically incorrect, and inconsistent system specifications.
- Code generators to generate executable code from pictorial system specifications.
- Documentation generators to produce the technical and user documentation required by structured methodologies.

CASE *toolkits* provide integrated tools for developers seeking to automate only one phase of the life cycle process, while *workbenches* provide integrated tools for automating the entire development process. *Frameworks* integrate CASE tools and/or link them with non-CASE software development tools, and *methodology companions* support a particular structured methodology and automatically guide developers through the development steps.

10.3.1 Well-Equipped
Toolkits

Toolkits can focus on the design of real-time, information, or project management systems. They can also be classified by the hardware and operating system on which they run; by the ease with which they can be integrated into a family of compatible CASE tools; by their architecture (open, so that they can be used with products from other vendors, or closed); by the structured methodology or methodologies they support; and by their development languages, such as, ADA, COBOL, FORTRAN, C, or PL/1.

Many CASE toolkits run on an IBM PC or compatible under DOS. Some run on the Apple Macintosh, Wang PC, or Texas Instruments Professional PC. Others only run on 32-bit workstations, such as the Digital Equipment Corporation (DEC) VAX Station II, or Sun or Apollo workstations; on an IBM or Data General mainframe, or across the DEC Vax family. Many open-architecture products are not limited to one specific hardware, operating system, target programming language, or structured methodology.

The analysis toolkit has four basic components: structured diagramming tools, prototyping tools, a repository, and a specification checker.

10.3.2 Structured Diagramming Tools

Structured diagramming tools are computerized tools for drawing, manipulating, and storing structured diagrams (such as data-flow and entity-relationship diagrams), which are required documentation for various structured methodologies.

Diagramming tools often reside on PCs or workstations that support graphics manipulation; at the minimum, they draw, update, and store data-flow and entity-relationship diagrams.

10.3.3 Prototyping Tools

Prototyping tools help to determine system requirements and predict performance beforehand. Essential to prototyping are user-interface painters—screen painters, report painters, and menu builders—that prototype the user interface to give users an advance view of how the system will look and to identify and correct problem areas. Screen dialog and navigation with data entry and edits can be simulated with or without compiles; source code for record, file, screen, and report descriptions, can be generated automatically.

Also essential are executable specification languages. These are the most sophisticated prototyping tools, which involve specifying system requirements and executing specifications iteratively to refine, correct, and ensure completeness of the system to meet user requirements.

10.3.4 The CASE Repository

The CASE repository is a design dictionary for storing and organizing all software system data, diagrams, and documentation related to planning, analysis, design, implementation, and project management. Information entered once can be maintained and made available to users who need it.

The repository stores more types of systems information, relationships among various information components, and rules for using or processing components than a standard data dictionary used in data management systems. The repository usually has many reporting capabilities, which gauge the impact of proposed changes on the system, identify redundant or unneeded data elements, and resolve discrepancies. System diagrams and dictionary entities are linked within the dictionary, and some CASE tools provide automated means of verifying entities for completeness and correctness.

10.3.5 Data Design Toolkits

These support the logical and physical design of data bases and files: logical data modelling, the automatic conversion of data models to third normal form, the automatic generation of data base schemas for particular data base management systems, and the automatic generation of program-code level file descriptions.

10.3.6 Programming Toolkits

Supported tools include hierarchical tree-structured diagramming tools with a syntax and consistency checker; a procedural logic diagrammer and on-line editor; a CASE repository with information manager; code generation; a test data generator; a file comparer; and a performance monitor.

A code-generating tool is especially useful because it automatically produces codes from a program design. CASE code generators can generate compiled, structured codes in languages such as COBOL, PL/1, FORTRAN, C, or ADA, manage program specification and design information, generate documentation, and support prototyping.

10.3.7 Maintenance Toolkits

The most useful maintenance tools include documentation analyzers—to read source code from existing systems and produce documentation; program analyzers—to evaluate execution paths and performance; reverse engineering—to identify the model upon which a system is based; and restructures—to enforce structured programming and documentation standards.

10.3.8 Project Management Toolkits

Automated project management tools can help project managers better track, control, and report on software projects, thus improving software development and maintenance. To be most effective, these tools should be able to access the CASE repository in the toolkit or workbench. Besides storing technical system information, the repository should be the central location for current status, estimation, budget, and quality-assurance information.

Some of these toolkits include tools for word processing; interfacing to electronic mail; spreadsheets; project-management forms; configuration management for change, version, and access control; project plans; a calendar and task assignment system; and estimation of time tables and scheduling.

10.4 DEMONSTRATED USE OF CASE TOOLS IN THE SDLC

CASE tools have demonstrated their usefulness in all three components of the CASE environment: planning, systems design, and systems development.

10.4.1 CASE in the Planning Environment

CASE tools gather information about: user problems and requirements; setting goals and criteria; generating alternative solutions.

They assist in: budget determinations; project duration and scheduling; manpower planning and scheduling; cost and time estimates; and project control.

10.4.2 CASE in the Systems Design Environment

CASE tools detail the design for a selected solution, including diagrams relating all programs, subroutines, and data flow.

They can generate data modelling and relationship diagrams, and also functional models.

The functional modelling and data modelling processes have tools to construct the appropriate types of design diagrams. Data-flow diagrams, program structure charts and entity-relationship diagrams are examples of diagrams.

10.4.3 CASE in the Systems Development Environment

CASE tools develop a construct or model of data base information about the physical data base schema and the requirements for building, testing, and checking data bases.

They produce language codes from definitions of data and processes stored in the data dictionary.

10.4.4 Samples of Output from CASE Tools

The next several pages illustrate the output from the three components of the CASE environment (see Figures 10.2–10.4).

The output illustrated in this example were produced from the following sample problem:

Sample problem. Our sample problem concerns a video rental store with the following:

- A customer rents tapes and makes rental payments.
- The Customer returns tapes, and may be assessed late charges of $1 per day.
- Overdue borrowers are to be notified.
- Tape rentals are to be reported.

- Store submits new tape
- Rate changes for the rental of some movie titles are to be posted.
- Customer address changes are to be listed.
- Customer requests for a particular movie title are to be listed.

Other details. The tapes involved are prerecorded video cassette tapes of movies, which can be rented. Each tape has a movie title and copy number. All copies of a movie have the same rental rate. Not all movies have the same rental rate.

A rental is the lending of a tape to a person in exchange for cash. A rental has a check-out date, a return date, and a rental charge. If a tape is late, there is a standard $1 per day late charge, to be paid upon return. A customer can rent more than one tape at a time.

The standard time period for a tape rental is two days. If the customer fails to return the tape in time, then a tape overdue notice is sent to the customer address, with the title and copy number and past-due return date listed.

A tape can be rented, on the shelf waiting to be rented, or overdue. This video store has no membership plan and doesn't take American Express. All transactions are in cash on-the-spot, no deposits are accepted.

10.5 SELECTION CRITERIA FOR CASE TOOLS

The ever-growing array of CASE tools makes it very difficult to decide which tool is best suited for a particular environment. This section attempts to ease that uncertainty by setting down a list of questions that the buyer should seek to get answers to, before buying a tool.

10.5.1 The questions

Is the tool a DBMS or dictionary software system? Dictionary and database management systems provide greater integration capabilities. As a result, CASE tools with these underlying structures have a greater capacity for sharing specifications across functions.

What is the future direction and functionality of the tool? When evaluating CASE tools, remember that CASE systems development is still in its infancy, so don't reject a tool with valuable attributes just because it does not currently have the full capabilities that you want.

Does the tool's manufacturer have an open-architecture philosophy? A manufacturer's willingness to share file formats with all viable, noncompeting CASE manufacturers means that you can move smoothly from planning through to systems development because you will be able to integrate specifications across CASE components. Moreover, you will have a healthy variety of options for CASE soft-

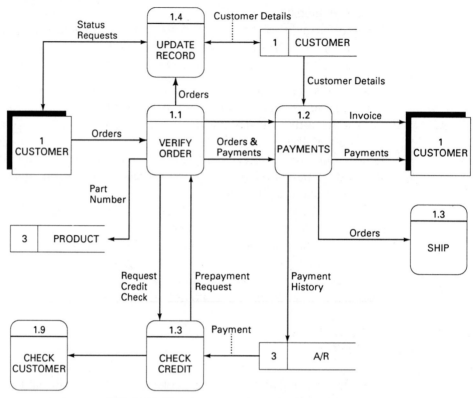

FIG. 10.2. Excelerator-produced data-flow diagram.

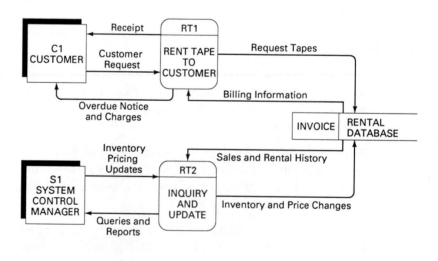

Rental System
Level 1 DFD

FIG. 10.3. Another Excelerator-produced data-flow diagram.

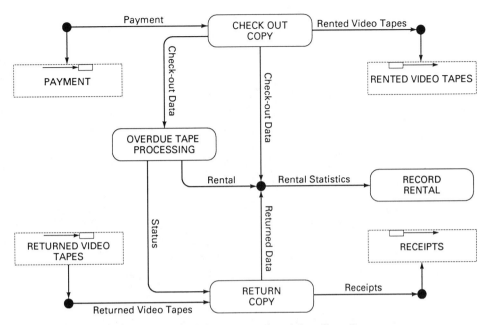

FIG. 10.4. Knowledgeware-produced data-flow diagram.

ware configurations. CASE manufacturers entering into exclusive hierarchical integration agreements with other noncompeting CASE tool manufacturers ultimately limits choice.

Does the CASE tool produce utility software that will read procedure and source libraries and create CASE component specifications for existing systems? The acquisition of CASE tools in a non-CASE environment creates a potential for inconsistencies in maintenance activities. Design and development specifications for systems designed and implemented before the installation of CASE components will not be consistent with those created after the installation of CASE tools. Thus, a multiplicity of maintenance activities will be necessary. Certain CASE tools offer utility software that will ready procedure and source libraries and create development specifications for existing systems, thereby mitigating the difference between pre-CASE and post-CASE systems documentation.

Does the tool have an effective interface to other CASE design tools already purchased or under evaluation? Often, several methodologies are used to design a system, so it is important that a CASE tool provide a healthy array of methodological techniques to use in the process. The dictionary entries must be capable of being shared across these methodologies, so the dictionary should be strong and versatile.

Does the tool have graphical methodologies capable of "exploding" design diagrams and dictionary specifications to a reasonable depth? Most of the CASE design tools provide graphical methodologies for representing proposed systems design. The graphical diagrams and the dictionary entries behind the components of the graphical diagrams must be capable of exploding to a reasonable number of lower, more specific levels.

Will the tool be capable of executing with windowing capabilities? An advantage of the windowing capability is that multiple portions of the design can be displayed simultaneously, and can therefore compensate for weaknesses in embedded explosion capabilities. As a result, the levels of explosion will not be restrictive and the comprehensiveness and integration of CASE design and development specifications should improve.

Does the planning model in the CASE planning component provide comprehensive coverage of corporate and functional unit strategic planning and systems planning? The planning component contains a model for representing the corporation and for use in determining the direction of the corporation and systems development. The strength of the CASE top-level components lies in the comprehensiveness of this planning model.

Does the tool provide a thorough means of prototyping? CASE development tools, rather than CASE design tools, provide the strongest prototyping methods. While it is not necessary that both types provide strong prototyping capabilities, at least one must provide this capability.

Will the tool soon be able to automatically generate first-cut physical design specifications from logical design specifications? The conversion of logical design diagrams into initial physical design diagrams should be automatic, because it simply involves the exchange and addition of graphical display table entries. While most CASE design tools currently do not offer this feature, ask your CASE vendor if the tool will offer it in the future.

Does the CASE design tool provide analysis support for design documentation? This concerns the capacity of the CASE tool to analyze design documentation and determine whether the specifications entered by the analyst conform to prescribed methological rules. The analysis should also indicate where design dictionary entries are incomplete. For example, a data flow diagram (DFD) with a freestanding block should be highlighted as violating one of the rules of structured methodology. In addition, blocks on a DFD not having corresponding dictionary entries should be highlighted.

Does the tool have the capacity to generate design specification reports automatically? The specifications created during logical and physical design activities serve as a source of documentation for the system. While they are permanently stored on disk devices, it is often advisable to get hard copy printouts of the design specifications for reference. Many CASE tools provide various report formats for this purpose, including the capability of indicating design flaws.

Does the lower-level CASE development component provide methods for convenience and comprehensive customization of the generated system? The CASE development component can already generate the major portions of the code systems. Systems development activity using CASE involves providing the customization of the generic code to fit the system. The custom specifications must provide comprehensive coverage of the system requirements. The generated programs must also be able to call on existing routines to prevent the system from "reinventing the wheel."

Does the tool permit distribution of design/development responsibilities? CASE design and development tools must provide a serviceable means of segregating job responsibilities and interfacing the individual efforts into a single system project.

Do the CASE design and development tools have the capacity to export portions of the design and development dictionary specifications? This is important, as design and development specifications for one system may be reusable in the design and development of other systems. "Reusable design" will join "reusable code" as a result of this capability.

Can the tool interface design and development specifications to the functional DBMS be used to maintain the company's data? It is rare to develop systems that are not affected by the data base environment, and the development of systems using CASE tools is not an exception. Therefore, it is important that the CASE tools be able to interface design and development specifications of applications systems to mainframe DBMSs and data base creation or modification.

Does the tool have word-processing capabilities? In addition to built-in word-processing capabilities, the tool should have an effective interface with standard word-processing systems. An added feature of some tools is the ability to pass documentation to a desktop publishing software system for more professional representation.

Does the tool enhance project management? The use of CASE tools does not preclude the need for effective project management. In fact, their use can enhance such management. Specifications that are entered using a planning component provide a boundary for design and development activities. This boundary provides a built-in means of determining when design and development activities diverge from originally planned specifications. Some CASE design and development tools can generate reports on the progress of individual project assignments, and some can interface to existing project management software systems. Currently, this interface is a temporary exit from the CASE tool into the project management system, but the interface will become much stronger in the future and provide more automatic updating of the project schedule.

Is it possible to modify the CASE design and development tools relative to your firm's internal or existing methodology? CASE tools are prepackaged systems and may need modification to make them more suitable for individual installations. Thus, it is important that the system have the ability to add or delete menu options or be able to modify the style of graphical or dictionary entry screens.

Can the tool automatically generate design, operations, and end-user documentation? As systems are designed and developed with CASE tools, documentation concerning components and users of the system are entered into the dictionary. Thus, the majority of design, operations, and user documentation required for documentation manuals is available from these dictionary entries. CASE systems should provide this documentation in either on-line or hard-copy form, with little additional work required from the project development team.

Does the tool have facilities for maintaining design as well as systems? When conditions in business warrant changes in the information systems function, the people responsible for maintenance should be able to effect the required system changes in the system's design specifications automatically. Alternatively, once those changes are made, the development tool should be able to designate where the current systems need changing, as well as to indicate which users need to be notified of the changes and what they need to be told. Some development systems already provide some of these capabilities. As the interface between CASE design and development software systems becomes stronger, modifications to design specifications entered into the design software will be able to modify development specifications, and, ultimately, the entire system. Since the planning component was the last to emerge, the interface between it and the design component is weak. Subsequently, as the interface between it and the design strengthens, it should have the same effect on those activities as the strengthening of the interface between design and development did.

Can the tool generate programs that span a range of systems? The hardware and software to create a transparent micro, mini, and mainframe environment are not far off. Consequently, the programs that the CASE tool generates must be able to provide the same execution services on a desktop micro as on a computer room's mainframe. Some of today's CASE development systems already offer this.

It goes without saying that the CASE tool manufacturer should be willing to provide a list of installations using its software and grant permission to contact them. This major criterion should govern the purchase of any software system. Should a software vendor refuse to supply this information, you have reason to doubt the validity and comprehensiveness of its product.

10.5.2 Analysis of Selection Criteria

A subset of the above questions were sent to about a dozen vendors of CASE tools. Their responses are recorded in an earlier text.

10.6 VENDORS OF CASE TOOLS

This section lists some of the major vendors of CASE tools and gives a brief summary of their products.

10.6.1 Vendor List

Adpac Computing Languages Corporation. Adpac develops, markets, and services technology support tools for the IBM mainframe operating under MVS. Adpac's CASE tools (DPDP and DESIGN) provide a front-end CAD/CAM diagramming technique that assists analysts in drawing any type of diagram, and in design analysis with the capability to verify the contents of diagrams.

AGS Management Systems Inc. AGS/MS is recognized as the world's leader in systems development methodologies and project management system. MULTI/CAM, the micro—mainframe CASE system created by AGS/MS, integrates software development tools, software design and production models, project management and any other user selected CASE tools into a unified, automated work environment.

American Management Systems. AMS is a major computer services firm specializing in applications development. AMS's Life-cycle Productivity System (LPS) integrates productivity tools from AMS and other vendors for strategic system planning, design, development, maintenance, and project management. LPS produces all output work products required by most methodologies. Major portions of LPS operate on PC's. Implementation, configuration control, and foundation software modules operate on the IBM mainframe.

Analysts International Corporation. Analysts International Corporation, a professional data-processing software and services company, and a leader in the computer industry for over 22 years, has introduced CORVET. CORVET is a graphics-oriented, PC-based, interactive CASE design and development product that generates stand-alone COBOL programs and comprehensive documentation for IBM mainframe environments.

Arthur Andersen & Co. FOUNDATION is a computer-integrated environment for software engineering developed by Arthur Anderson & Co. Covering the entire systems development life cycle, FOUNDATION consists of METHOD/1, a PC LAN-based tool for planning and design, and INSTALL/1, an IBM mainframe-based environment for implementation and support of DB2 applications.

Arthur Young & Co. Arthur Young is an international accounting, tax, and management consulting firm, which is working with KnowledgeWare to develop the Information Engineering Workbench (AY/IEW), markets KnowledgeWare products internationally, and uses the AY/IEW for systems building. Arthur Young can demonstrate its experience-building systems using the AY/IEW and information engineering techniques.

ASYST Technologies, Inc. The DEVELOPER provides multiuser, automated support for the systems development process, through its repository located either at the PC, at the mainframe (using DB2), or at both sites. The DEVELOPER and its CUSTOMIZER module allow the use of any methodology at all levels of compliance and rigor. Repository integrity is maintained through a menu-driven SQL query language and build-in ASYSTants capabilities.

Bachman Information Systems, Inc. Bachman Information Systems, Inc. is exhibiting The Bachman Product Set, which supports the development of new applications while supporting existing applications. It provides the powerful maintenance, enhancement, and migration capabilities MIS departments need to control the largest component of their workload.

CATALYST. CATALYST, an information technology firm of Peat Marwick, has created PATHVU, RETROFIT, ReACT, and DataTEC. PATHVU provides analysis and detailed reporting of program logic and structure. RETROFIT restructures COBOL code. ReACT translates Assembler programs to structured CO-BOL. DataTEC provides data element analysis, standardization, and migration capabilities. These products make up the reengineering baseline necessary to migrate existing systems to advanced technical environments.

CGI Systems, Inc. PACBASE is a full-cycle CASE product. It integrates mainframe- and PC-based analysis and design workstations for the development and maintenance of application specifications. This is done through active prototypes, a centralized enterprise-wide dictionary that controls and manages all business specifications directly into complete COBOL applications, including all code and documentation.

Chen & Associates, Inc. Chen & Associates provides products, training, and consulting in data-oriented system development. Their products (PC-based) are ER-Designer, which defines information requirements in entity-relationship diagrams; SCHEMAGEN, which generates schemas for data base systems (from micro-based to mainframe based); and Normalizer, which normalizes data or words.

Computer Sciences Corporation. The Technology Activity's Design Generator is an object-oriented expert system that automatically selects a central transform from a data flow diagram and generates an initial design represented in structure chart notation. The graphic-intensive user interface features intelligent pop-up menus and multipane browsers.

Cortex Corporation. CorVision is an applications development system that automates the entire software development cycle for the DEC VAX/VMS environment, using a technique called Picture Programming. Picture Programming allows DP professionals to visualize an application by diagramming the design, and then automatically generating a production-ready application directly from the pictures.

Digital Equipment Corporation. As a leading manufacturer, Digital provides a range of integrated Application Development tools for solutions to business and engineering problems. The offerings are workstation-based and address all aspects of the applications development life cycle. They are integrated into the VAX hardware, software, and network architecture to provide enterprise-wide solutions.

ETECH Algorithms and Systems, Inc. ETECH SOFTROBOT is an intelligent workbench built on the PSDDL (Problem Statement and Diagram Description Language). ETECH-D is a fully automatic diagramming toolkit without screen editing. ETECH-M is an intelligent project manager driven by Project-Makefile, ETECH-R reusing language, and ETECH-G language-independent code generator based on reusability. It can reach many professionals' goals.

Holland Systems Corporation/Deloitte Haskins and Sells. Deloitte Haskins and Sells and Holland Systems Corporation have pooled their consulting and software product expertise in the IRM area. The result is a line of products that address the entire information resource management process . . . from business modelling . . . to data base design and analysis . . . to applications development and implementation. The companies feature the 4Front Family of IRM products.

I-Logix, Inc. I-Logix, Inc. pioneers system design automation with STATEMATE a tool that models the dynamic behavior of real-time systems as well as system functions and architecture. With STATEMATE. users produce a specification that is compiled, allowing its execution to be viewed on screen. STATEMATE includes three graphic languages for modelling, execution, and simulation capability; rapid prototyping in Ada; and 2167A documentation.

Index Technology. Index Technology markets the Excelerator family of products that automate systems development. Products include PC PRism, for systems planning; Excelerator and Excelerator/RTS, for analysis and design, plus links to application generators and programming environments. Excelerator and Excelerator/RTS support a variety of techniques and methodologies and can be tailored for each organization's needs.

Infodyne International, Inc. InfoDyne markets and distributes MASTER, a PC-based CASE tool and methodology, based on the E-R (Entity-Relationship) approach to systems planning and design. MASTER accommodates numerous approaches to the problem of the analysis, design, and documentation of all design activities relating to the conceptual, logical, and physical models of data and internal processes in an information system.

Inforem PLC. Inforem's Professional Application Generation Environment

(PAGE) is a unique CASE offering. A multiuser product, it combines on-screen graphics with a systems encyclopedia and uses a relational data base on networked PCs. PAGE is based on the Inforem Method, which provides a seamless transition right from analysis to program code both for PC and mainframe systems.

Integrated Systems, Inc. AutoCode focuses on the needs of real-time software engineers, and addresses all steps from analysis to design, stimulation, and code generation. The graphical specification environment features engineering block-diagrams, data flow/control flow, state transition, and process descriptions. Ward-Mellor real-time software methodology with Boeing-Hatley extensions are included in an environment where simulation and analysis can be performed for design verification; also, real-time code in C, Ada, or Fortran can be generated automatically.

Interactive Development Environment (IDE). IDE's product, Software through Pictures, is a set of integrated graphical editors and error-checking tools supporting structured analysis and design methods. The editors are linked to a data dictionary supporting the definition of names, types, constants, associated text. Users can generate Ada declarations and define process and module templates to generate specifications.

James Martin Associates. James Martin Associates, an international consulting firm, is considered a leader in creating systems development methods and CASE tools to support those methods. With more than 250 professionals throughout the world, JMA's teams provide commercial and government clients with technical and management services.

Knowledgeware, Inc. Knowledgeware, Inc. provides a complete Integrated Computer-Aided Software Engineering (I-CASE) environment for the planning, analysis, design, construction, and maintenance of computer-based information systems. The Information Engineering Workbench (IEW) provides enterprise modelling, data modelling, process modelling, systems design, and code generation experts. The "Knowledge-Coordinator/Encyclopedia" team uses state-of-the-art artificial intelligence technology.

Language Technology. Language Technology provides CASE products for the IBM mainframe market. The company's flagship product, RECODER, is a leading COBOL structuring tool. RECODER automatically transform difficult-to-maintain, unstructured COBOL into structured COBOL. Language Technology's INSPECTOR is the only quality-assurance tool based on a scientific measurement of COBOL quality and maintainability.

Manager Software Products (MSP). The MANAGER Family of products (PC and Mainframe) is dedicated to automating all phases of the systems life cycle, from strategic information planning to the generation of enabled code. MSP has created managerVIEW, the intelligent workstation-based graphical information engineering tool, driven by the central knowledge base resident in the corporate dictionary. ManagerVIEW is integrated with the mainframe corporate dictionary, and also runs on the IBM PC family and PS/2.

Michael Jackson Systems, Ltd. Jackson CASE tools automate the widely acclaimed Michael Jackson methods of system development and program design. SPEED-BUILDER supports the analysis phases of development through powerful graphical and text facilities, and automates documentation production. The cooperating Program Development Facility (PDF) generates complete, well-structured program code from Jackson structure charts.

Micro Focus. Micro Focus COBOL/2 Workbench puts a mainframe programming and testing environment on a PC platform under MS-DOS or OS/2. It is used by developers of COBOL, CICS DL/I, and IMS DB/DC applications to improve productivity and cut applications development backlogs. Micro Focus COBOL compilers and CASE tools are the choice of IBM, AT&T, Sun Microsystems, Microsoft, and others.

Nastec Corporation. Nastec develops tools for commercial, government, engineering software developers. CASE 2000 DesignAid is based upon an interactive, multiuser data base, with features for process modelling, real-time system modelling, and documentation. Operating in the IBM PC and Digital VAX environment, CASE 2000 also includes tools for requirements management, project management and control, and consulting and training in CASE technology.

NETRON Inc. The NETRON/CAP Development Center is a CASE system for building custom, portable COBOL software using a frame-based software engineering process called Bassett Frame Technology. NETRON/CAP unifies the prototyping/development/maintenance life cycle into an automated specification procedure. The open design architecture allows unlimited automation of additional application functionality for IBM mainframes and PCs, VAX systems, and Wang VS minis.

Optima, Inc. (Formerly Known as Ken Orr & Associates). Optima, Inc. integrates the use of tools and technology with the experience of people. DSSD (Data Structured Systems Development), the flagship product, is a life cycle methodology that serves as the base of the product. CASE tool products that automate the methodology are Brackets, for the diagramming process, and DesignMachine, for requirements definition and logical data base design.

On-Line Software International. On-Line Software International has created CasePac—automated software development with a powerful DB2 data dictionary. As the foundation for On-Line Software's CASE platform, CasePac provides a complete, fully active central repository, and software engineering facilities including a graphics front end, change management, and maintenance facilities.

Pansophic Systems, Inc. Pansophic Systems, Inc. has created TELON. The

TELON application development system captures design specifications to generate COBOL or DL/I applications. TELON assists in the transition from analysis to design by providing interfaces to leading front end analysis tools. TELON components include directory, data administration, screen/report painters, prototyping, specification facilities, automated documentation, a generator, and a test facility.

POLYTRON Corporation. POLYTRON offers a configuration management system for MS/DOSPC and VAX/VMS software development. PVCS maintains versions and revisions of software systems. PolyMake automatically rebuilds any desired version of the system. PolyLibrarian maintains libraries of reusable object modules. The tools work together or independently with any language and your existing tools.

Popkin Software & Systems Inc. Popkin Software & Systems offers SYSTEM ARCHITECT, a PC-based CASE tool running under Microsoft Windows. Its set of process- and data-driven methologies for structured analysis and design include DeMarco/Yourdon, Gane and Sarson, Ward & Mellor (real-time), structure charts, and entity-relationship diagrams. SYSTEM ARCHITECT's data dictionary-encyclopedia utilizes the dBase II file format.

Ready Systems. Ready Systems has created CARDTools, which supports automatic DoD 2167 documentation generation, and specific Ada requirements, including object oriented design, packages, information hiding, and rendezvous. CARDTools offers real-time performance deadline analysis on multitasking architectures, and hardware/software interface specification including intertasking synchronization and communication designs, allowing for design analysis verification prior to actual implementation.

Sage Software, Inc. Sage Software, Inc. develops, markets, and supports a family of CASE tools for developers of IBM-based information systems. The company's product family (known as the APS Development Center) encompasses the software development cycle and supports the physical design, interactive prototyping, coding, testing, and maintenance of COBOL-based applications software.

Softlab, Inc. Softlab, Inc. has created MAESTRO, an integrated software engineering environment. MAESTRO organizes and manages the software cycle through real-time project management, time accounting, and individual standards. MAESTRO integrates customizable tools for design; coding, testing, documentation, and maintenance; it is language independent; and it fits in numerous hardware and software environments.

Tektronix. TekCASE is a family of automated software development tools that help software engineers and project managers analyze, design, document, manage, and maintain complex real-time systems. Because they support Digital's complete VAX line and integrate with VAXset software, TekCASE products are flexible, extensible, and especially well-suited for large projects.

Texas Instruments. Texas Instruments' integrated CASE product, The Information Engineering Facility, is designed to automate the complete systems development life cycle. It consists of a powerful mainframe encyclopedia and PC-based graphical toolsets to support analysis and design. TI can demonstrate the major components of this product, including: strategic planning, analysis, design, CO-BOL code, and data base generation.

The CADWARE Group, Ltd. The CADWARE Group, Ltd. designs, produces, and markets rule-based frameworks and modelling tools for the development of complex systems. Managers, planners, systems analysts, and designers can use these tools to help manage the complexity of defining and evaluating mission-critical business, industrial, and technical systems.

Transform Logic Corporation. Transform addresses the development and maintenance of the entire application life cycle. Using expert system technology, complete COBOL applications are produced for IBM mainframe DBMS's DL/I and DB2. The concepts behind automated development, data-driven design architecture, prototyping, and maintenance are reviewed, with examples of user accomplishments.

Visual Software, Inc. Visual Software, Inc. markets personal CASE tools for workstations, LAN, and mainframe design environments. The base package, vsDesigner, is a methodology-independent workbench supporting shared access to LAN-based information repositories. Several default design syntaxes come with the product, including those for real-time design. Extensive analyses are supported, and an optional SQL interface to the design data is available.

YOURDON Inc. The YOURDON Analyst/Designer Toolkit supports both the traditional and real-time YOURDON Techniques, and allows for the creation of all of the diagrams associated with these techniques. The diagramming facilities of the Toolkit are integrated with a powerful project dictionary, which features dBase III compatibility. The Toolkit provides error checking to insure the accuracy of diagrams and dictionary entries.

10.7 GETTING CASE IN PLACE

There are three basic steps for implementing CASE technology in a software development organization:

- Determine the methodology and automation support requirements.
- Select a CASE product.
- Implement the CASE product.

This is a lengthy process involving numerous people, so major results should not be expected for a couple of years. Even then, the biggest and longest-term benefits may come in application maintenance. CASE tools make it much easier to maintain specifications.

10.7.1 Determine the Methodology

Following agreement on the organization methodology, whether data-flow or entity-relationship diagrams, the next step is to determine what is most needed in automation support. For a larger organization, with complex applications, some of the following capabilities may be desired:

- Interactive drawing of analysis diagrams.
- Automatic data normalization.
- Consistency checking.
- Initialization of the physical design from requirements.
- Prototyping tools.
- A directory of reusable code modules.
- Analysis methodology enforcements.
- An interface with the application development environment.

A second key decision is whether a single-integrated environment or a CASE front-end to a more classical development environment is desired.

10.7.2 Select a CASE Product

Once methodology has been determined and a decision made as to which CASE capabilities will be useful, it is necessary to select a product. This may be done on the basis of:

- Which environment is to be used in—PC or mainframe?
- What applications does the tool support? Some tools support a specific data base (e.g., DB2) or language (e.g., Ada).
- Does the tool support the available methodology?
- Is the vendor financially secure? It is always good to talk to people who have experience using the vendor's CASE tool.

10.7.3 Implement the CASE Product

An aggressive strategy for CASE implementation in smaller organizations is to automate many software engineering techniques simultaneously on a small trial project. The basic steps are as follows:

- Select a new development project to be used for the CASE trial situation.
- Staff the trial project with the best requirements and design analysts.
- Assign a full-time CASE administrator to learn the tool, make detailed methodology decisions, enter information, run analysis reports, and generate specifications.

A large organization, with thousands of users nationwide, must take a different approach. Most such organizations will find it physically impossible to decide on a complete automated methodology and then get hundreds of people trained on it in a short time period.

In this circumstance, a method or support group acts as the change agent, introducing a few techniques at a time and supporting them with automation.

10.8 SUMMARY

This chapter introduced a tool that has literally "taken the software development world by storm." CASE tools are making a big impact on software development and will continue to do so for years to come.

The chapter introduced the topic of "what are CASE tools?" and showed how they could be selected and used in small or large organizations.

11

Business Systems Planning—Strategic Data Planning

11.1 INTRODUCTION

Although information systems may provide intended results, many companies give little thought to the potential value of serving overall corporate objectives with systems capable of sharing data among executives and departments. Piecemeal systems development leaves many organizations with numerous nonintegrated, inflexible information systems. Nor has any thought been given to the information needed to support managerial decision making and strategic planning; instead, the purpose of most of today's automated information systems is to enhance operational control or transaction-processing activities.

It has been estimated that the typical organization without a corporate-wide data model spends approximately 80 percent of each systems development dollar to restructure existing applications programs and data files to keep up with changing information needs. Also, an organization may be depriving itself of a major competitive advantage it it fails to manage its information processing resources efficiently and creatively.

The best way to avoid the problems associated with the traditional approach to developing information systems is to adopt a formal systems planning methodology. This is a predetermined process by which the senior executives in an organization supply input that can be used to translate the organization's strategic goals into a detailed information systems development plan for achieving those goals. The next several sections of this chapter will discuss such a plan.

11.2 THE BUSINESS
SYSTEMS PLAN

The Business Systems Plan (BSP) was first made available to customers in 1970. BSP is defined as a structured approach to assist an organization in establishing an information systems plan to satisfy its short- and long-term information needs. BSP is a way to translate business strategy into information systems strategy.

Some objectives of BSP include:

- Impartially determining information systems priorities.
- Planning long-lived information systems based on enduring business processes.
- Managing systems resources to support business goals.
- Assigning systems resources to high-return projects.
- Improving user department and information systems department relations.
- Improving the understanding of the need to plan information systems.

The BSP methodology's major premise is that organization-wide information systems should be planned from the top-down, and implemented piece by piece from the bottom-up. Top-down planning means that a group of top executives provides a study than consisting of managers, professionals, and information systems experts with the broad strategic objectives of an organization, as well as other important information. The study team systematically composes them into an architecture of information systems that will support the organization's strategy.

The BSP methodology consists of six major activities:

- Developing the BSP.
- Documenting the business objectives.
- Defining the business entities.
- Defining the information architecture.
- Reporting the findings to management.

11.3 DEVELOPING
THE BSP

The most important activity of the BSP is to develop a plan for conducting the BSP study. The plan should cover what the objectives of the study are, how the study will be conducted, who will participate in the study, and the expected output from the study. A typical plan will contain the following:

- The goals of the study.
- The scope of the study.
- Problems addressed by the study.
- What the study will do for the organization.

- Output from the study.
- The study team.
- The interviewees.
- The timetable for the study.

11.3.1 The Goals of the Study

The goals of the study are broad statements indicating what will be accomplished by the undertaking of the study. For example, the defined goals of the BSP study could be as follows:

- Establish an MIS Systems Plan, which will be synchronized with, and in support of, the organization's business goals and strategies.
- Provide an overall data architecture and applications system architecture for the organization.
- Provide system implementation strategies.
- Provide action plans and resource requirements for the implementation strategies.

11.3.2 The Scope of the Study

The scope of the study sets the boundaries for the study. It indicates what will or will not be included in the study. For example, for an organization located in one area, the scope may indicate what departments of that organization will or will not be included in the study. For an organization spread over several geographically diverse areas, the scope may indicate that only the head office, and not the branch offices, will be included in the study.

11.3.3 Problems Addressed by the Study

This section of the plan establishes the reasons for conducting the study. It details problems that currently existing in the MIS area of the organization. Although existing problems are highlighted, no solutions are offered at this time. Some of the problems that may be highlighted for an organization are as follows:

- MIS projects experience cost and/or schedule overruns.
- Complaints are often made about the quality, timeliness, and effectiveness of MIS service.
- Applications systems are not congruent with the organization's business goals and are brought into line only with great difficulty and expense.
- Senior management feels that MIS is not effectively under its control. It cannot understand why projects: are so big; take so long; Require such large staff; and are so expensive.

- Maintenance projects are utilizing almost 80 percent of the manpower.
- Many applications systems are old and out of date. They do not meet current company needs.
- New products cannot easily be added to the organization's systems.

11.3.4 What the Study will do for the Organization

This section of the plan further strengthens the objectives of the study and identifies some of the tangible results of the study. Some of these results are as follows:

- The study provides identification of business opportunities for employing information technologies.
- The study indicates that BSP will provide a data architecture that constrains the design and development of new information systems, so that all information systems will be consistent with one another.
- The study indicates that BSP will provide a framework within which trade-off decisions can be made between short-term investments and long-term ones.
- The study indicates that BSP supports company-wide 'top-down' systems design, but will allow for 'bottom-up' piece-by-piece implementation, which will be made necessary by the realities of budget constraints, limited resources, and the drive for short-term results.

11.3.5 Output from the Study

The main output from the study will be a comprehensive report that will detail an overall data architecture and applications system architecture for the organization, system implementation strategies, and action plans and resource requirements for the implementation strategies.

11.3.6 The Study Team and Interviewees

The composition of the study team is critical to the success of the study. The team should be made up of high-level management, preferably on the vice-presidential level; users, at the department head level; and senior MIS personnel.

The interviewees should be senior executives who are knowledgeable about the mission, goals, and objectives of the organization. They should be personnel with a ranking no lower than the vice-presidential level.

11.4 CONDUCTING THE BSP STUDY

There are approximately 13 major steps to perform in conducting a BSP study. Two of them, gaining executive commitment and preparing for the study, precede the study itself. All of the steps are important; although some can be carried out to varying degrees, none can be completely eliminated. The following subsections summarize the steps and their significance for senior executives.

11.4.1 Gaining Executive Commitment

A BSP study must not begin without a commitment from a top executive sponsor. In addition, other executives must be willing to become involved in it. Success depends on the degree to which these executives can supply the study team with other views of the organization and its data needs.

A key part of this firs step is the concurrence of all parties regarding the effort's purpose and scope. Differing expectations are common and can lead to disappointing results and unmet expectations. Furthermore, the purpose of the study is to commit the organization to a course of action based on recommendations made at the study's end; therefore, early expectations are critical.

The choice of the team leader follows. The team leader may or may not be the executive sponsor: in some cases, the sponsor will feel comfortable leading the study, but in others, a different manager is more appropriate. The team leader will direct the study team full time for the six to eight weeks that the team typically requires. A team of four to seven members is recommended. The leader must be in a position to ensure that the team members have access to other important executives and must properly interpret members' thoughts and ideas.

The team members must be prepared to 'sell' the study to executive sponsors and the interviewees. The 'selling' effort must address:

- The purpose and scope of the study.
- Some of the problems that will be addressed by the study.
- What the study will do for the organization.
- The identification of the team members who will work on the study.
- The identification of those who will be interviewed.
- The time commitment required of each executive involved.

11.4.2 Preparing for the Study

Everyone should know the BSP plans and procedures before the study is conducted, so that executives can provide *optimal* input and the study team can make *optimal* use of the input. Study team interviewees should be identified as soon as possible so that their interviews can be scheduled. Information on the organization's basic business functions and its current data processing configuration should be compiled during this phase to facilitate the team training and orientation. The team should be given exclusive use of a conveniently located control room where study activities can be conducted. By the end of this phase, the team should produce a study control book, containing:

- A study work plan.
- A list of executives to be interviewed and an interview schedule.
- A schedule for reviews with the executive sponsor at certain checkpoints.
- An outline of the final report.
- Business and information systems data, analyzed, charted, and ready for use in the study.

The executive sponsor should review the accomplishments made during this phase, before the actual beginning of the study.

11.4.3 Starting the Study

The BSP study begins with three presentations to the study team:

- The executive sponsor repeats the purpose of the study and its anticipated output.
- The team leader reviews business facts already collected so that each team member is thoroughly up to date.
- The senior information systems executive discusses the department's recent activities and problems, so that the study team members understand the departments current role in the organization.

11.4.4 The Enterprise Analysis

This is the most important phase of the BSP study. Here, the study team identifies the current and accurate organization structure; the business strategies that exist to enable the organization to achieve its mission, goals, and objectives; the business processes or logically related decisions and activities that are required to manage the resources of the business; and the data classes or entities. This step is important, because failure to define the strategies and processes properly will be reflected in all information that follows.

11.4.5 Define Business Strategies

Business strategies are provided by the executive management team. The target output from this step should be a list of four to eight goals and approximately five strategies per goal. A sample list of strategies follows:

- Improve inventory control.
- Streamline the customer order cycle.

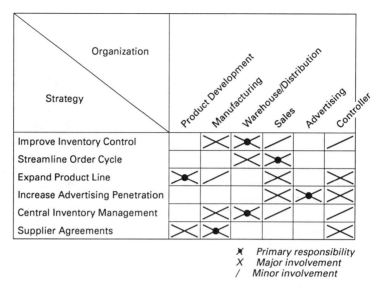

FIG. 11.1. Strategy versus organization matrix.

- Tie the production schedule closer to customer demand.
- Manage inventories centrally.
- Reduce losses due to bad debts.
- Reduce raw material expenses by supplier agreements.
- Increase advertising penetration.
- Expand selling relationships with major department stores.

The study team may expand these strategies to a form that will produce the major processes for the study. For example, the strategy "Improve inventory control" may be expanded to read: "Develop a more comprehensive system for tracking information as to what items are located in each warehouse and where they are within the warehouse."

The next step in this phase is to produce a "Strategy versus Organization" matrix. An example of such a matrix is shown in Figure 11.1.

11.4.6 Define Business Processes

Business processes may be defined as a group of logically related decisions and activities significant to the enterprise. During this phase, the study team seeks to define a set of processes that are in place in the organization. The target output from this step is a list of 40–60 business processes. The criteria for selecting these processes are that the process should be:

- Independent of organizational structure.
- Significant to the enterprise.

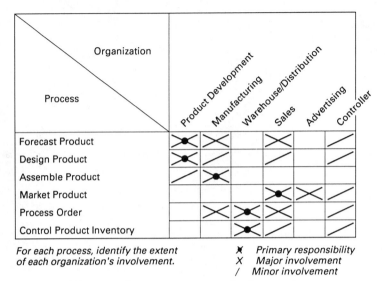

For each process, identify the extent
of each organization's involvement.

✗   Primary responsibility
X   Major involvement
/   Minor involvement

FIG. 11.2. Process versus organization matrix.

- Named by verb–object.
- Nonredundant activities and decisions.
- Able to be aggregated or disaggregated.
- Unique for each enterprise.

The study team develops a "Process versus Organization" matrix from the data collected during this phase. An example of this matrix is shown in Figure 11.2.

In order to prioritize any information strategy opportunities, the study team also develops a "Process versus Strategy" matrix. An example of this is shown in Figure 11.3.

11.4.7 Define Data Classes

During this phase, data is grouped into related categories called data classes or entities. The future information systems architecture will include data bases that contain this data. The organization of these data bases should minimize the need for future revisions. Criteria for data categorization are the relationships of the data to the business processes.

The study team will develop three matrices for the defined data classes. They are as follows:

1. Matrix Usage—Process versus Data Class. This matrix:

   - Reflects company-wide data needs.
   - Communicates data-sharing by processes.
   - Aids in defining the application scope of data classes.

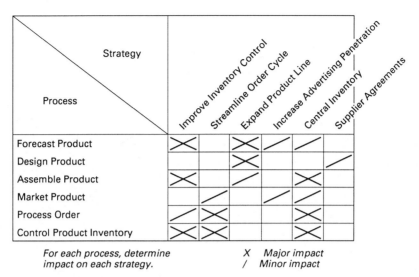

For each process, determine   X   Major impact
impact on each strategy.   /   Minor impact

FIG. 11.3. **Process versus strategy matrix.**

- Aids in identifying application interdependencies.

2. Matrix Usage—Strategy versus Data Class. This matrix illustrates the relative importance of data regarding each entity to the business strategies.
3. Matrix Usage—Organization versus Data Class. This matrix:

- Is used to define the focal point of responsibility for data about an entity.
- Is used to help interviewees define their data requirements.
- Identifies data-sharing possibilities.

Figures 11.4, 11.5, and 11.6 illustrate examples of these matrices.

11.5 CONDUCTING EXECUTIVE INTERVIEWS

The major purpose of this phase is to validate the understanding that the team has developed thus far. Another purpose is to achieve the commitment and support of executives not yet deeply involved in the study. The executive interviews conducted during this phase provide the study team with the basic understanding of the business problems that the future information systems architecture should solve.

11.5.1 Preparation for Interviews

The success of the interviewing process depends to a large extent on the amount of preparation that has gone into conducting the interviews. Preparation for the interviews should include:

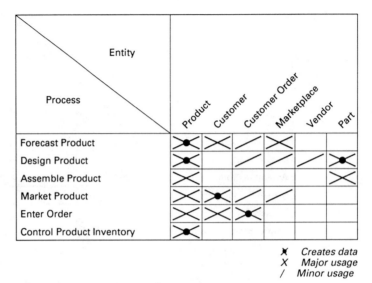

FIG. 11.4. **Entity versus process matrix.**

- Verifying the interview list with the corporate sponsor.
- Scheduling interviews.
- Developing an interviewee briefing.
- Developing a letter to be issued to each interviewee by the corporate sponsor.
- Developing questions, tailored to each interviewee, that will be asked.
- Obtaining and preparing an interview room.

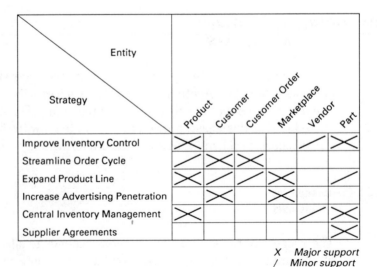

FIG. 11.5. **Entity versus strategy matrix.**

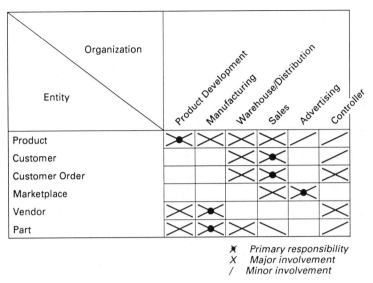

FIG. 11.6. Entity versus organization matrix.

- Selecting an interview team.
- Assigning roles to each team member.
- Preparing and rehearsing the roles of each team member.

11.5.2 Conducting the Interviews

The interview process and the questions asked during the interviews are specifically geared toward obtaining information from the executives about their involvement in the strategies, processes, and data requirements of the organization. During the interviews, the team will do the following:

- Brief the executives on the objectives, activities, and output of the study.
- Indicate the purpose and flow of the interview.
- Elicit information opportunities by addressing the interviewee's need for support for:
  - A particular business strategy involvement.
  - The processes for which the interviewee is responsible.
  - The data classes that satisfy the interviewee's business functions.
  - The interviewee's critical success factor.

The interviewee should be asked to give a value and priority ranking for each information opportunity. The interviewee should also be asked to state expectations for the future and any additional information opportunities that these expectations might entail.

11.5.3 The Post-Interview Process

After the interviews are completed, the interview team will:

- Complete the information opportunities details.
- Compile notes and create summaries.
- Send summaries to interviewees for corrections and/or comments.

11.6 INFORMATION OPPORTUNITY ANALYSIS

The purpose of this phase is to analyze the information opportunities that were discovered during the interviews. It is also during this phase that the study team will develop the necessary support recommendations and prioritize them.

The information opportunities are reviewed for duplication. They are then categorized by process and by data class. This categorization will allow for the identification of applications and the data classes to support each information opportunity. The applications will be prioritized in order to determine a sequence for implementation.

11.7 THE DATA AND PROCESS ARCHITECTURES

The study team will use the processes and data classes identified earlier in the study to design data bases of the future information architecture. The architecture for the processes and data classes will vary from organization to organization. It may consist of a simple list of data entities and their relationships, or of entity-relationship diagrams at the highest level for the data architecture. A list of the processes and their functions, or a data flow diagram, may suffice for the process architecture.

The study team will identify major systems and subsystems and determine whether some subsystems must be completed before others. The architecture diagrams will reflect the relationships of systems and subsystems.

11.8 DEVELOPING RECOMMENDATIONS AND ACTION PLANS

The study team will make recommendations not only for systems, subsystems, hardware, and software, but also for adjustments to systems under development and to systems currently in production. Another major area for recommendations includes strengthening information systems management with improved planning and control mechanisms identified during the study. The action plan will identify priorities and the means of delivering the future information architecture.

11.9 THE FORMAT OF
THE FINAL REPORT

A brief executive summary covers the purpose of the study, its methodology, its conclusions, and its recommendations. A more detailed and comprehensive report expands these topics. In addition, an oral presentation to executives with slides or other visual media should conclude the study.

The report content should be as follows:

1. Executive Summary
2. Background

   - The study objectives
   - Methodology

3. Business Perspective

   - The business environment
   - The mission, goals, and strategies

4. Findings

   - The enterprise model
   - Information opportunities/needs
   - Information management requirements

5. I/S Strategies and Recommendations

   - Prioritization criteria
   - I/S strategies and Recommendations

6. Action Plans
7. Appendix

11.10 CONSEQUENCES OF NOT
DOING A BSP STUDY

There is considerable argument for and against doing a BSP study. There has been sufficient discussion in these pages as to why a BSP should be done. However, the consequences of not doing a BSP study should be stated in a very general way.

One of the most important outputs of a BSP study is the data architecture or model showing what data the organization needs to do its business. Unfortunately, many organizations are finding that the old systems do not fully support their business functions. For example, the billing function may not support the aging of accounts receivables or itemize line items on a bill. The lag in registering a client for health insurance or terminating that client may be costly to the health insurer.

Further, the system may not support functions across departments. A good data architecture built on the collection of pertinent processes, functions, and problems from the entire organization will go a long way to better serving the corporate needs of the organization. With the BSP study completed, and the data architecture in place, the organization can avoid spending millions of dollars on systems that become obsolete in a few short years or even before they are developed. The organization can now prioritize their systems development based on its needs.

During the conducting of a BSP study for a major organization, one manager lamented that, because the records are not in sync with a major health care agency, very often when they terminate clients, these terminated clients continue to receive health care benefits from other providers and the organization has to pick up the tab for the service. A proper data architecture can prevent this occurrence.

11.11 SUMMARY

The Business System Plan (BSP) described in this chapter was developed by IBM. The author reported on this plan with very little departure from the BSP course normally given by IBM. The readers are recommended to augment their knowledge gained from this chapter with courses from IBM.

PART 3

CONTROL OF THE DATA BASE ENVIRONMENT

12

Data Base Security, Privacy, and Integrity

12.1 INTRODUCTION

Data Security is defined as the procedural and technical measures required to:

- prevent any deliberate denial of service.
- prevent unauthorized access, modification, use, and dissemination of data stored or processed in a computer system.
- protect the system in its integrity from physical harm.

The access control requirements are particularly important in time-shared and multiprogrammed systems, in which multiple users must be prevented from interfering with each other and users must be prevented from gaining unauthorized access to each other's data or programs.

Privacy is an issue that concerns the computer community with maintaining personal information on individual citizens in computerized recordkeeping systems. It deals with the right of the individual regarding the collection of information in a recordkeeping system about his person and activities and the processing, dissemination, storage, and use of this information in making determinations about him.

Integrity is a measure of the quality and reliability of the data on which computer-based information systems depend. Many computerized data bases in use today suffer from high error rates in the data they receive, and consequently are riddled with bad data and with incorrect data, making even the most efficient and sophisticated system is well-nigh useless.

Computer privacy is concerned with the moral and legal requirements to protect data from unauthorized access and dissemination. The issues involved in computer privacy are therefore political decisions regarding who may have access to what and who may disseminate what, whereas the issues involved in *computer security* are procedures and safeguards for enforcing the privacy decisions.

Privacy issues affect all aspects of computer security because of legislative measures enacted. With due consideration of its social implications, legislation for computer privacy determines the types of information that may be collected, and by whom, the type of access and dissemination, the subject rights, the penalties, and the licensing matter.

In 1973, the Department of Health, Education, and Welfare proposed several actions that should be taken to help protect individual privacy. This report proposed the following fundamental principles of fair information practice to guide the development of regulations and laws concerning privacy.

- There must be no personal-data recordkeeping systems whose very existence is secret.
- There must be a way for an individual to find out what information about him is in a record and how it is used.
- There must be a way for an individual to prevent information about him obtained for one purpose from being used or made available for other purposes without his consent.
- There must be a way for an individual to correct or amend a record of identifiable information about him.
- Any organization creating, maintaining, using, or disseminating records of identifiable personal data must assure the reliability of the data for their intended use and must take reasonable precautions to prevent misuse of the data.

Guidelines and procedures may be established for accountability, levels of control, type of control, rules, and checklists. Preventive measures and recovery due to internal threats and external intrusions are also a part of data security. For these threats and intrusions, the causes, effects, and means must be studied. More difficult aspects of data security research include risk analysis, threat analysis, assessment, and insurance. By knowing the risks involved, data security may be expressed in terms of quantitative indicators, cost factors, and options. These discussions are included in the following section.

12.2 CONDUCTING A THREAT ANALYSIS

A threat is defined as that which has the potential to menace, abuse, or harm. A threat can either modify or destroy the functional purpose of an object, and hence is a source of potential danger. In the context of the discussion of threat analysis and data security, a threat shall be expressed as the danger to which data is exposed.

A threat analysis is defined as the methodology employed to assess the level of the system's security and the protection mechanisms in place to counter the threat. Threat analysis is also useful in designing cost-effective security systems.

A good threat analysis is an important element in the review of security needs. Together with an analysis of vulnerability, it provides the basic data needed to assess the risks. Even if threats are not expressed in probabilistic terms, their existence should be recognized and priority ratings should be assigned.

The threats considered in this chapter will be limited to those faced by the data. Threats to physical security, which are usually countered by the installation of some physical measures, will not be considered. In this category of threats are fire hazards, illegal entry into a specific computer installation, and hardware failure.

The methodology most frequently used and employed in the studies that produced most of the data for this chapter is the checklist method. This approach consists essentially of a series of questions asked to determine what protection measures are in place to counter threats against specific objects.

Considerable attention should be devoted to planning the questionnaire and the follow-up interviews with respondents. The researcher should set specific objectives and have clearly measurable goals for each associated task. The scheduling and coordinating of interviews with the various respondents should also receive considerable attention.

12.2.1 Threat Analysis Case Study

The threat analysis detailed in this subsection was conducted in a data base environment using IMS as the data base management system (DBMS). The objects selected for the study included:

- The Program Specification Blocks (PSB) library.
- The Data Base Description (DBD) library.
- The Application Control Block (ACB) library.
- The data dictionary.
- Source and object modules for COBOL, Mark IV, and the Application Development Facility (ADF).
- Cobol Message Processing Programs (MPP).
- Data files.

The primary goal of the questionnaire was to determine what protection exists to counter the following categories of threats:

- Unauthorized access to the library.
- Unauthorized manipulation of the members of the library.

- Unauthorized users browsing the library.
- Unauthorized use of utility routines.
- Inadequate auditing and monitoring of threats.
- The obtaining of access to the data base by bypassing the PSB library.
- Illegal use of processing options.
- Destruction of the storage medium.
- Unauthorized distribution or exposure of the libraries.
- Unauthorized copying or altering of the libraries.
- Illegal deletion of stored data.
- The passing of sensitive data by authorized users to unauthorized users.
- Unauthorized copying or altering of the library.
- Access to residues of data.
- Unauthorized use of terminals.
- Collusion of employees.
- Denial of access to system resources.
- Inadequate documentation and historical change data to establish audit trails.
- One programmer having sole knowledge of access to, and maintenance responsibility for, sensitive programs.
- Inadequate training and attitudes towards data security.
- Exposure of sensitive data following abnormal ending of a job.

An example of a typical question found on the questionnaire follows: Does the computer give a dump of memory if an abnormal end of job occurs during the running of a sensitive program?

The response to the several questionnaires were then analyzed to determine the level of protection available to each specific object.

12.2.2 Analysis of Results

The results obtained from the responses to the questionnaire agreed favorably with results from similar surveys. They indicated that the following threats existed:

- Inadequate authentication of user identification.
- Inadequate controls over the use of utilities and special-purpose programs.
- An inability to identify terminals and users in the event of a breach of security.
- A need for risk assessment.

Some of the major systems surveyed required identification for access to data that depended on personal knowledge of corporate structure, a manager's position code, or a manager's signing authority, and, in general, on information that can easily be obtained by corporate customers. The ease with which such information could be obtained presented considerable security problems.

In view of the ease of obtaining such information, the authentication process should be stringent enough to provide some protection for the passwords, user identification, or sign-on identification. The authentication process should not be based on further personal knowledge of the authorized user. For example, requiring a user to give the birthdate, name of first child, or high school attended as authentication for an already weakened identification scheme only serves to further weaken the system.

The unauthorized user armed with such easily obtainable knowledge of the authorized user will be in a position to pass the authentication requirements with little difficulty.

It was demonstrated that it was possible for an authorized user to retrieve a user's source program and alter the code without detection. The unauthorized user could illegally embed statements in the user's code, recompile the code, and return the object code to the load library.

Existing controls did not restrict (by, for example, a user profile) access to a user's source libraries by other users. A user profile would restrict that user to certain libraries, programs, or portions of stored data.

In a similar manner, control should exist over certain specialized routines, utility programs, and programs that allow specially trained programmers to bypass standard procedures to gain access to stored data. Administrative controls should be in place that outline what procedures one should follow to gain access to routines and utilities. These controls should include who can authorize the use of such programs, signatures required, logs to be completed, and any follow-up reporting that should be done.

The responses to the survey showed that there was almost no ability to make a positive identification of a terminal or its user in the event of a security breach. The failure was due to the following:

- Inadequate authentication.
- The use of logical terminals identifications.
- Inadequate audit trials.

The protection mechanism to counter this threat should include restricting the use of certain terminals to certain types of transactions, certain terminals to processing during certain periods, and include in the authentication process certain transformations that require keys that would link the terminal to the corresponding identity.

Finally, the analysis of the responses reveal that consideration should be given to some or all of the following protection mechanisms:

- Frequently changing passwords.
- Levels of authority and processing functions.
- Automatic terminal sign-off after a period of inactivity.

- A fixed time to bring up terminals and period processing.
- On-line auditing—one terminal being used to maintain monitoring and surveillance.
- Dedicated telephone lines.
- Encryption of files.
- Administrative control of utilities.
- Erasure of residues on tapes/disks.
- A log of all terminal users.
- Hardwired terminals for entering specific transactions.
- Individual libraries—users are restricted by either password or user identification to libraries for which they have authorization

12.2.3 Conducting a Risk Assessment

Another useful exercise, in addition to conducting a threat analysis, in implementing security safeguards in an organization is to conduct a risk assessment.

A risk assessmentis an analytical process designed to quantify the data security required by an organization. It considers the threats to data and the loss that would occur if a threat were to materialize. The purpose of a risk assessment is to help an organization establish priorities for cost-effective safeguards to reduce the probability of given threats or aid in recovery from a loss.

For some potential threats, a risk assessment may show the potential loss to be catastrophic to the organization. In some cases, when a security breach can be evaluated in terms of cost, delay, disclosure, or other measure, establishing a base level of security may be a desirable first step.

The risk analysis provides a rational approach toward choosing security safeguards. A security program should logically provide protection in the most economical manner.

The following questions, therefore, should be answered in the course of a risk assessment:

- What are the specific results desired; that is, exactly how much security is required?
- What is the proper balance between security program cost and potential benefits?
- When trade-offs can be made between protection and recovery, how much effort should be expended on each?

Several full-length checklists and questionnaires for conducting risk assessment are available in current literature on the subject. The author developed a questionnaire as part of data base security research conducted during the past five years. This questionnaire is illustrated as Exhibit A.

Exhibit A.
User Risk Analysis
for

_____ *System*

Prepared by _____

Origin Date _____

1. Uses of the Application Output (List)

    A. _____

    B. _____

    C. _____

    D. _____

2. Dependencies. Are there other uses of the Application Output outside of your specific area? Please list.

    USE   USER

    _____   _____

    _____   _____

    _____   _____

3. Critical Dates of Time Periods. Please list any critical dates or time periods (e.g., fiscal year end, Christmas checks).

    Date   Reason   Brief Description

    OF: _____   Criticality

4. Dollar Risk versus EDP Application Outage Duration. Please complete Table I (attached).

5. Critical Files.

    A. Please list critical files.

    _____

    _____

    _____

    _____

    B. File backup requirements.

    Are the files backed up by EDP resource?   _____
    If so, how often?   _____
    How are the files backed-up:
    a) Magnetic tape in vault.   _____
    b) Microfim.   _____
    c) If microfilm, where stored?   _____

    d) Estimate time to recover if microfilm or listing is only backed-up   _____
       partially?

    e) If back-up is by microfilm, how often is it updated?   _____

6. Revenue Estimate. Revenue earned is _____ per _____ .

7. Fall-Back Model.

   A. Is a manual fall-back system feasible?

     a) If so, how long to put it in place?   _____

     b) Cost to put it in place?   _____

     c) Estimated running cost of the manual system is

      _____ per _____ .

   B. Time frame when manual fall-back system ceases to be feasible?   _____

   C. Estimated loss as a result of interruption. Please complete Table II.

8. Remote Access System Data. Is the application run remotely from the
   computer center?   _____

   If yes:

   A. What type of terminal is used _____

   B. Is your terminal connected to the computer via:
     a) leased lines.
     b) Dial-up plus accoustic coupler.
     c) Other (State).

    _____

    _____

   C. Is your terminal in the same building as the computer?   _____

   D. Do you use a password to sign in on the system?   _____
     If so,
     a) Who determines the password (User/Technical Branch)?   _____
     b) How?   _____
     c) How often will passwords be changed and by whom?   _____
     d) Would you change the password when an employee that knows the
       password terminates his/her employment?   _____
     e) Houw many people know the password?   _____

   E. Would you consider the information transmitted/received over the
     terminal   _____
     a) Business confidential?   _____
     b) Personally private?   _____
     c) Information whose dissemination should be controlled?   _____
     d) Information to be used in making management decisions?   _____
     e) Information that may be disseminated to anyone within a
       department without control?   _____

F. Do you employ any cryptographic methods to protect vital data? If so:
   a) Are software or programmatic techniques used? _____
   b) Are hardware devices used? _____
      If so, name the manufacturer and model number

      _____

   c) The cryptographic methods are used because of:
      I) Pertinent legislation _____
      II) User priorities _____
      III) Other _____

G. What programming languages can you utilize from your terminal? Please list and encircle those not required _____

H. Which of the following security measures pertaining to terminals have you considered adequate for your needs?
   a) Nondisplay screen mode for entering the sign-on parameters and update passwords.
   b) The defined terminal access be restricted to a particular time of day?
   c) The defined terminal to be automatically signed-off after extended periods of inactivity?
   d) In the case of attempted violations, the system identifies the responsible terminal/user?
   e) The transaction can only be entered from the terminals so authorized?

I. Security Audit Report(s).
   Please indicate reports applicable to this application:
   a) RACF
   b) Access matrix model
   c) Generated from DBMS log tapes
   d) Security audit trail

J. Other Potential Problem Areas Not Covered Above

TABLE I. Risk (in Dollars) versus EDP Application Outage Duration.

Outage Duration	Dollar Risk	Reason for Risk	Time*	Cost*	Remarks
1 Day					
2 Days					
3 Days					
4 Days					
5 Days					
6 Days					
7 Days					
2 Weeks					
3 Weeks					
4 Weeks					
2 Months					
3 Months					

*Time—Time when you would start manual.

TABLE II. Estimated Business Lost (Revenue) as a Result of Interrupted or Degraded Service.

Duration	Revenue Lost (in Percent)	Revenue Lost (in Dollars)	Critical Time*	Remarks
1 Day				
2 Days				
3 Days				
4 Days				
5 Days				
6 Days				
7 Days				
2 Weeks				
3 Weeks				
4 Weeks				
2 Months				
3 Months				

*Duration—Duration of interruptions of degredation.

12.2.4 Achieving Data Base Privacy

Privacy of information in a data base is lost either by accidental or deliberately induced disclosure. The most common causes of accidental disclosures are failures of hardware and the use of partially debugged programs. Improvements in hardware reliability and various memory protection schemes have been suggested as countermeasures. Deliberate efforts to infiltrate an on-line data base can be classified as either passive or active.

Passive infiltration may be accomplished by electromagnetic pickup of the traffic at any point on the system.

Active infiltration—an attempt to enter the data base to directly obtain or alter information—can be overtly accomplished through normal access procedures by:

- Using legitimate access to the data base to ask unauthorized questions, or to browse in unauthorized data.
- Masquerading as a legitimate user after having obtained proper identification by other means.
- Having access to the data base by virtue of your position.

The above spectrum of threats can be countered by a number of techniques and procedures. Some of these were originally introduced into time-shared, multiuser systems to prevent users from inadvertently disturbing each other's programs, and then expanded to protect against accidental or deliberately induced disclosures of data. In the following discussion, some of these countermeasures are cited.

12.2.5 Access Management

These techniques are aimed at preventing unauthorized users from obtaining services from the system or gaining access to its files. The procedures involved are authorization, identification, and authentication. Authorization is given for certain users to enter the data base and request certain types of information. Any user attempting to enter the system must first identify himself and his location, and then authenticate his identification.

12.2.6 Privacy Transformations

Privacy transformations are techniques for coding the data in user-processor communications or in files to conceal information. Privacy transformations consists of sets of logical operations on the individual characters of the data.

Privacy transformations break down into two general types, irreversible and reversible.

Irreversible includes aggregation and random modification. In this case, valid statistics can be obtained from such data, but individual values cannot be obtained.

Reversible privacy transformations are as follows:

- Coding—A word in one language replaces a group of words in another.
- Compression—This removes redundancies and blanks from transmitted data.
- Substitution—Letters from one or more items are replaced.
- Transposition—All of the letters in the clear text appear in the ciphered text, but in a distorted sequence.
- Composite transformation—Represents combinations of the above methods.

12.2.7 Cryptographic Controls and Data Transformation

Cryptographic transformations have long been recognized to be an effective protection mechanism in communication systems. In the past, they have been used mainly to protect information that is transferred through communication lines.

There is still much debate as to the cost/benefit of encrypting large production data bases. The author's experience with encryption indicates that, because of the need to produce clear text from large encrypted data bases, the cost of this type of control makes it prohibitive.

12.2.8 Data Base Integrity

A data base integrity system is used to prevent certain types of inconsistencies introduced by errors of the users or their applications programs from affecting the contents of the data base. By enforcing semantic restrictions on the information, it is possible to insure that the contents of the data base is correct and that no inconsistencies exist between related information and original information. The increased use of data dictionaries has gone a long way toward ensuring the integrity of data bases.

The data dictionary documents what validity and edit rules are to be applied to the data.

These rules can be classified into a few basic categories that correspond to specifications of range, sets of values permitted, format, uniqueness of some values, nonmissing values for a field, and interfield assertions.

Systems surveillance, measurement, and auditing are critical elements in providing the technical base for adequate integrity.

The effectiveness and operability of the entire system, especially the protection mechanisms, must be continually scrutinized and measured. Management must also be able to detect and respond to events that constitute system security threats.

Finally, the introduction of a properly functioning audit system should allow the internal auditors to indicate that the occurrence of certain events should trigger audit trails that cannot be destroyed deliberately.

13

Development of Security Controls

13.1 INTRODUCTION

This chapter discusses some features of data base security, privacy, and integrity beyond a level that the author considers introductory. The features are termed advanced because they are features that a worker, wishing to install security mechanisms in his organization, may select for direct implementation. The chapter does not give a step-by-step approach to the implementation of these features, but discusses the issues that a security analyst must consider when deciding to implement security measures.

The chapter starts off by discussing top level management involvement in data base security, privacy, and integrity. The author has discovered that one of the main causes of inadequate data base protection, or no protection, in several organizations is due to the fact that top level management does not see the need to incur the cost of protecting the data base contents. The analyst who wants to pursue the integration of security measures at his installation must first convince management of the need for security and get their support, not only during the implementation of the measures, but for constant monitoring of the performance and adequacy of the measures and the upgrading of those measures as warranted.

In order to determine the adequacy of existing security measures, the level of protection required for the data base content, and the cost to install these measures, the analyst must conduct a risk analysis. The need for a risk analysis and the risk analysis itself is discussed in later sections of the chapter.

The chapter concludes by discussing some protection mechanisms that may be implemented by organizations to achieve data security.

Protection mechanisms may be defined as the controls implemented by the organization to achieve data security and protection. The mechanisms discussed in this chapter can be divided into two categories. There are those mechanisms or controls that are implemented external to the computer system and operating software, and those implemented as part of the operating or management systems software. Administrative controls would fall into the category of external protection mechanisms, whereas the following controls could be considered to be internal protection mechanisms:

- Auditing and monitoring the data base.
- Authorization schemas, such as in access control matrix.
- A Resource Access Control Facility (RACF).

13.2 TOP LEVEL MANAGEMENT INVOLVEMENT IN DATA BASE SECURITY, PRIVACY, AND INTEGRITY

The author's years of research in data base security, privacy, and integrity revealed that one of the major reasons for the non-effort or failure of data base security efforts in most corporations is the lack of involvement and support by the top level management.

It could be assumed that, with the overwhelming statistics relative to the ease with which computer systems are penetrated, and the resulting loss, that management will support a program to provide adequate security. However, this assumption is not necessarily valid.

For one thing, most managers are inundated with immediate problems. The one thing they feel they do not need is to be further burdened with hypothetical problems. But security deals with hypothetical problems (i.e., things that might happen).

Further, these are things that management hopes will not happen. And they involve "bad" human behavior, in most cases, while managers prefer to deal with "good" behavior such as how employees can get their work done more efficiently, get company problems solved, and increase company profits.

The net result, as one might expect is that security considerations tend to be postponed. They are postponed, that is, until some serious consequence occurs from a breach of security. Then there may be a flurry of excitement, as an attempt is made to bolster security measures.

Management's willingness to consider the security problem is the most important single factor in the whole security program.

For one thing, management makes the critical decision at the outset as to whether the security problem will be approached. They must set the policies, ground rules, and scope of the security project. They create the reviews to determine whether things have changed to the point where major new protective measures must be considered.

Management sets the guidelines and procedures for an effective system of internal controls. These controls deal with handling the assets and liabilities of the organization. They identify the sensitive data and programs that need to be protected. They classify and itemize the existence, importance, or need for protection.

Further, these assets and liabilities can be protected, in part, by protecting information about them. For example, if a fictitious payment transaction is entered into the accounts receivable data base, an asset is lost. Also, if a fictitious invoice is entered into the accounts payable data base and is paid, an asset is lost. If a manipulated transaction causes a valuable piece of property, a vehicle, or piece of equipment to be written off as salvage, and is taken by some unauthorized personnel, an asset is lost. Protection against these threats is accomplished by controls set up by management that make it difficult to enter such fictitious transactions into the system. Management support for a security program may be in any of the following forms:

- Assignment of major responsibilities for the program.
- Organization and assignment of the team for the security program.
- Setting policies and general control objectives.
- Undertaking a cost/benefit study to determine what protection features to implement.

Management can set the desired tone for the whole security program by identifying those general standards that it wishes to emphasize by the following means:

- The study of existing protection to point out where additional or improved protection is needed.
- The design and installation of the needed protection, under the responsibility of operating management.
- Checking the effectiveness of the whole internal protection system by means of periodic audits.

13.3 ADMINISTRATIVE CONTROLS

Administrative controls may be defined as management policies formulated to ensure adequate maintenance of a selective access program, whether it be selective authorization to data files or physical areas. They may include the development and implementation of security policies, guidelines, standards, and procedures.

Effective administrative controls can go a long way in helping to ensure that an organization has a secure operating data base environment. These controls will certainly assist in reducing or eliminating both deliberate and accidental threats. Once an intruder realizes that the chances of being detected are good, the intruder may be deterred from attempting to breach the security. This determination of the probability of being detected can be made from knowledge of the existing administrative controls. For example, if the intruder knows that there is a requirement for the user's name and terminal log-on times to be recorded, then the intruder will very likely not use the terminal.

The probability of accidental threats succeeding decreases with an increase in the user's knowledge of the operating environment and requirements. Clear and precise administrative procedures and assertions help to increase that knowledge and in turn decrease the probability of successful accidental threats.

Administrative controls, and security features in particular, should be developed in parallel with the actual systems and programs development. A group consisting of internal auditors, the development team, and users should be assigned to develop these controls and standards.

Administrative controls can be defined in the following areas:

- Top-level management decisions—decisions pertaining to the selection and evaluation of safeguards.
- Security risk assessment studies to identify and rank the events that would compromise the security of the data base and the information stored in it.
- Personnel management—pertaining to employee hiring and firing procedures, employee rules of conduct, and enforcement.
- Data handling techniques—a well-defined set of rules describing the precautions to be used and the obligations of personnel during the handling of all data.
- Data processing practices—including the methods to control accountability for data, verification of the accuracy of data, and inventories of storage media.
- Programming practices—pertaining to the discipline employed in the specification, design, implementation, programming coding, and debugging of the system.
- Assignment of responsibilities—assigning each individual a specific set of responsibilities toward carrying out certain security functions for which that individual is held responsible.
- Procedures auditing—an independent examination of established security procedures to determine their ongoing effectiveness.

13.4 AUDITING AND MONITORING THE DATA BASE

Auditing and monitoring are integral features of data base security. Should an intrusion be attempted, the system must be able to detect it and react effectively to it. Detection then implies that the system has a threat monitoring capability. Threat monitoring requires the following actions:

- Monitoring the events of the system, as related to security.

- Recognizing a potential compromise to the security system.
- Diagnosing the nature of the threat.
- Performing compensatory actions.
- Reporting the event.
- Recording the event.

While threat monitoring is an active form of surveillance, an equally important, but more passive form, is the auditability of the data base. A security audit should be able to cover the past events of the system and, in particular, cover all security-related transactions.

Audit trails that can lead to the identity of users, terminals, and authorizing bodies should be a feature of all applications.

The monitoring process within an organization should include the ability to determine whether:

- The controls over the data base administration function are effective.
- The process by which sensitive data is determined is adequate.
- The procedures by which security violations are detected are in place and effective.
- The extent to which data access is restricted to only authorized individuals is workable.
- The ability to restrict access by a program to data, other programs, and libraries exists.
- Terminal security features such as log-on, log-off, and restart are adequate and effective.
- The procedures to follow during processing interruptions are effective.

The importance of keeping records and logs of events affecting the data base and its environment cannot be overemphasized. The events recorded should include performance data, all error or abnormal events, all transactions related to sensitive information, and all overrides of the established system's controls.

Several data base management systems provide logging capabilities as part of their package. These logs should be investigated for their adequacy and ability to meet the auditing requirements of the environment. Organizations should not be hesitant to design and implement their own in-house logging facilities if the manufacturer's prove inadequate.

Any security effort in an organization should eventually involve internal auditors. This involvement becomes mandatory due to the changing requirements for evaluating and verifying controls in a secure data base environment.

Personnel responsible for security can offer considerable assistance to the auditors in determining the accuracy, integrity, and completeness of systems.

Researchers are now suggesting that the internal auditors become involved in the development stages of a system, and not only in the post-installation evaluation. The auditors' experience should provide the development teams with insight into the various methods they can use to approach their responsibilities in controlling and auditing the total information processing system.

Because of the rapidly changing data base technology, internal auditors need to constantly upgrade their skills. Systems development teams with current knowledge should assist the auditors in filling the gaps in their knowledge of techniques and concepts of integrated data base system design.

The development teams should strive to increase management's awareness of changes in the data processing environment, as they effect internal audit and the controls governing data processing.

Finally, the following list of management activities should enhance the internal auditing capabilities within a corporation, and especially as they effect the data base environment:

- Ensure that all staff realize the importance of internal auditing in the security effort.
- Issue a clearly defined internal audit mandate that specifies the responsibility of internal audit as it relates to all phases of the security effort.
- Clearly define the working relationship among users, internal auditors, and development teams responsible for data base security, privacy, and integrity.
- Encourage the development of new techniques and internal audit approaches to ensure the security, privacy, and integrity of the data base.
- Require the development of security control guidelines.
- Ensure that internal auditors participate in the security effort.

13.5 TYPES OF PROTECTION MECHANISMS

In an earlier section, I introduced two classes of protection mechanisms. There are those built into the computer operating system (internal mechanisms) and those not linked to the operating system (external mechanisms). The next subsections of this chapter will discuss some of those protection mechanisms in more detail.

13.5.1 The Access Matrix as a Protection Mechanism

The access matrix is an internal protection mechanism built into the operating system. It is essentially a set of tables that indicate who has access to what data. The access matrix consists of the following components:

- Objects that are to be protected.
- Subjects seeking access to these objects.

- Different protection levels for each object.
- Rules that determine how the subjects access each object.
- A monitor that mediates all access of a subject to an object.
- Directories containing information about the objects and subjects. The information on the object consists of such things as the unique identifier, protection level, types of access permitted, and data types. The information on the subject consists of the unique identifier and class of subjects.

The interaction between the subjects and objects can be represented by an access control matrix (see Table 13.1). The protectable objects are the row-components of the matrix. The subjects seeking access to the objects are the column-components of the matrix. Each entry in the access matrix determines the access rights of the subject to the object and is defined as the access attribute in the model.

The access matrix model is dynamic enough to include any class of objects or subjects within the data processing environment. It can provide a high level of protection for any object irrespective of whatever application the organizations' personnel develops and runs against the integrated data base.

Each object will be placed in a class determined by the level of protection required for that object. Each subject will be a member of a hierarchy. The hierarchical classifying of the subjects will allow subjects to create other subjects while ensuring that the created subject will not have more privileges than its creator. Some of the subjects that will be considered in the model are as follows:

- Database administrator.
- Development teams.
- System and applications programmers.
- Maintenance.
- Operations.
- Terminals.
- Programs and utilities.

Some of the objects that will be considered in the model are the:

- Programs and utilities.
- Terminals.
- Database files.
- OS files.
- Data base segments.
- Data base fields.
- Data dictionary entries.

The access matrix—case study. A typical case of an application of the access matrix is shown below.

TABLE 13.1. A Typical Access Matrix.

Emp. Name	Emp. Address	Emp. Phone #	Emp. S.I.N.	Emp. Education	Emp. Salary History	Emp. Medical	Emp. Pension	
11	11	11	11	11	11	11	11	Personnel
01	01	01	01	00	00	00	01	Accounting
00	00	00	00	00	00	00	00	Marketing
00	00	00	00	00	00	00	00	Purchasing
11	11	11	11	11	11	11	11	Data Base Administrator
10	10	10	10	10	10	10	10	Maintenance
11	11	11	11	11	11	11	11	Data Base Administrator
10	10	10	10	10	10	10	10	Maintenance
10	10	10	10	10	10	10	10	Programmers
10	10	10	10	10	10	10	10	Operations
01	01	01	00	00	00	00	00	Clerical

Legend: 01 = Read; 11 = Read and Write; 00 = No access; 10 = Write only.

Each entry in the access matrix in Table 13.1 determines the access rights of the subjects to the objects. For example, the 01 in the first column and second row indicates that the Accounting department can *read* the Employee Name; the 11 in the first column and row indicates that the Personnel department can both read and write to the Employee Name on the Employee data base; the 00 in the fifth column and second row indicates that the Accounting department can neither *read* nor *write* to the Employee Education information; and the 10 in the first column and sixth row indicates that the Maintenance department can only *write* to the Employee Name on the Employee data base.

The matrix can accommodate several other access attributes such as *execute, delete, update, append* (add something to the end of a data item without altering its original contents), *sort, create,* and *own.* This can be accomplished by adding appropriate codes.

The elements of the access matrix usually contain bits that represent accesses which can be performed by the subject on the object. If desired, however, the elements may contain pointers to *procedures, directories,* or *programs.* This feature is useful since programs or procedures contain greater processing capabilities than a simple *write* command, for example.

The additional processing information from the procedures, directories, or programs will be made available at each attempted access by a given subject to a given object. The information will allow those access decisions that depend on information not easily represented in the access matrix to be made.

13.5.2 Rules Governing Accessing Decisions

The accessing decisions are governed by a set of rules, which are listed below:

- A subject is permitted to transfer any access attribute that it holds for an object to any other subject.
- A subject is permitted to grant to any other subject access attributes for an object that it owns.
- A subject is permitted to delete any access attribute from the column of an object that it owns or the row of a subject that it created.
- A subject is permitted to read the portion of the access matrix that it owns or controls.
- A subject is permitted to create a nonsubject object. The creation of an object consists of adding a new column to the access matrix. The creator of the object is given 'owner' access to the newly created object, and may then grant access attributes to other subjects for their object.
- The owner of an object is permitted to destroy that object. This corresponds to deleting the column from the access matrix.
- A subject is permitted to create another subject. This consists of creating a row and column for the new subject in the access matrix, giving the creator 'owner' access to the new subject, and giving the new subject 'control' access to itself.
- Only the 'owner' is permitted to destroy a subject. This corresponds to deleting both the row and the column from the access matrix.
- Access based on the access history of other objects is permitted; a subject A may write to object F only if the subject has not read from object G.
- Access based on the dynamic state of the system is permitted; subject B may read from object H only at a time when the data base in which the object resides is in a predetermined state.
- Access based on the prescribed usage of the object is permitted; a subject may sort an object in a protection level higher than that of the subject, provided no date is returned to the subject.
- Access based on the current value of the object is permitted; a given subject may not read the salary field of any personnel record for which the salary value is greater than $20,000.
- Access based on the class of certain subjects is permitted; no access to a certain object can be made by a class of subjects between certain time period (e.g. between 12AM and 8AM.
- Access based on the class of certain objects is permitted; certain terminals or portions of the data base can't be accessed between 12AM and 8AM.

The access matrix is really the heart of the security system. By including more information in it, complex aspects of data security such as data-dependent checks, can also be achieved.

13.5.3 Protection Levels of Access Matrix

In the access matrix described in the previous subsection, authorization to access an object is based on the *protection levels* of the objects and the classification of the subjects. Access requests are denied unless the classification of the subject requesting access equals or exceeds the protection level of the object requested.

Access can be controlled beyond the file level of the data base if desired. By using directories that allow access to other directories and eventually to actual files, hierarchies of successively more restrictive access can be set up. This approach will provide adequate protection at the field level of the data base.

The protection level of each object will be determined by the team that does the risk analysis. Each protection level will then be assigned to a *directory*. The movement of an object from one directory to another will indicate that the protection level of that object has been either increased or decreased.

The protection levels of the model will be increased as the need for more security is uncovered. Some levels that may be considered are as follows:

- No sharing at all (complete isolation).
- Sharing copies of programs, files, or the data base.
- Sharing originals of programs, files, or the data base.
- Sharing entire programming systems.
- Permitting the cooperation of mutually suspicious systems.
- Providing subsystems with the ability to perform a task, but guaranteeing that no secret records of or from that task are kept by subsystems.

13.5.4 The Access Matrix Monitor

The monitor of the access matrix is that part of the software that ensures that there is no violation of the protection levels of the objects. It should be designed in such a way that any attempted violation of the protection levels or the data base will trigger an audit or logging capability. In order to accomplish this, the designer must ensure that there can be no unauthorized alteration of the monitor.

The monitor can either be some software mechanism or administrative controls that validate and then permit or deny each and every request for access to protectable objects.

A security program is effective to the extent that it reaches and affects all elements of the organization. One of the most effective mechanisms for assuring widespread distribution and uniform enforcement of security policy is through an existing or newly created standards program. A good standard can be defined as a precept that is enforced because the benefits outweigh the costs.

When initially developing a computer security program, it is essential that meaningful policy and standards be set forth and disseminated to all personnel, so that each individual is fully aware of mandatory security requirements.

As a minimum, these standards should address the following areas:

- The background of the security policy.
- The purpose of the security policy.
- Responsibilities for security.
- Personnel security.
- Physical access controls.
- Media and facility protection.
- Communication and network security.
- Hardware and software.
- Password control.
- Control of the release of sensitive data.
- Integrity controls and error detection.
- Security violation.

Before dissemination to the organization as a working document, standards must be fully coordinated among the various organization departments.

Procedures are more definitive: They provide step-by-step direction in performing a course of action. They should be specific and oriented to a given task in a given department. Security procedures should be detailed enough to be usable as a working document. For example, procedures regarding password changes should read "passwords will be changed by system administrator at least once per month," and not "passwords will be changed regularly."

In any organization, probably the most difficult aspect of security procedure is enforcement. It is one thing to declare that programmers will not leave on-line terminals unattended, but quite another problem to enforce the rule. In this regard, security procedures should be subjected to the three rules of effectiveness:

- Economic feasibility—are the procedures too costly?
- Operational feasibility—a ten-digit password might be secure, but is it a reasonable solution?
- Technical feasibility—can the procedure be implemented with the existing technical knowledge and equipment?

13.5.5 Administrative Controls in the Access Matrix Environment

The organization about to use the access matrix should develop policies and standards that will form the basis of the administrative controls that can assist the access matrix in its efforts to deny or grant access to protectable objects. If adequate controls exist, attempts at unauthorized access may be thwarted before the computer system is entered.

Interviews should be conducted with data security personnel to determine what procedures are already in place to control subjects' requests to resources.

All aspects of the requesting process should be examined, and the adequacy of the existing controls evaluated. It is hoped that the study will lead to new controls that will reflect the current environment and the need for adequate data security.

13.5.6 The Software Version of the Access Matrix Monitor

The monitor, that part of the access matrix model which enforces the security policy, should be designed according to the following three principles:

- Complete mediation—the monitor must mediate every access of a subject to an object.
- Isolation—the monitor and its data base must be protected from unauthorized alteration.
- Verifiability—the monitor must be small, simple, and understandable, so that it can be completely tested and verified to perform its functions correctly.

13.5.7 Design of the Monitor

Some considerations in the design of the monitor are as follows:

- There must be an interface between the monitor and other parts of the system, such as user programs.
- There must be an explanation as to how control is to be passed across the interface—in terms of invoking or calling the monitor.
- There must be means of identifying processes that interact with the monitor.
- There must be means of queuing and assigning priorities for requesting services of the monitor.
- There must be an interface of the monitor with other auditing programs.
- Protection of the monitor against modification must exist.
- There must be an interface of the monitor with subject and object directories

13.5.8 Functions of the Monitor

The main functions of the monitor can be listed as follows:

- It is responsible for creating and deleting subjects and objects.
- It creates a process containing the subject ID, the object's protection level, and associated access attributes.
- It terminates the subject's process and cleans up on the subject's behalf.
- It releases all reserved objects, closes any objects that are opened, removes

the subject from the request queue, and purges the portion of memory that acted as the work area.

- It maintains data consistency and seeks to avoid or resolve data interference.
- It reserves and holds objects.

13.5.9 The Design of Subject and Object Directories

The directories to be established for the access matrix model will include the following:

- Information on subjects.
- Information on objects.
- Protection levels.
- Pointers to other directories.

13.6 OBJECTS AND SUBJECTS OF THE ACCESS MATRIX

The subjects of the matrix should be members of a hierarchy and have functions in relation to that hierarchy. For example, the DBA could be the universal subject and function with the ability to:

- Establish new subjects.
- Impose logical limits on the resources.
- Remove a subject's ability to access the data base.
- Determine the maximum protection level of each subject.
- Define the resource limitation of each subject.
- Monitor and display all subjects and the protection levels of objects.
- Reclassify a subject.
- Reclassify an object.

The objects of the matrix must have a unique identifier, access attributes, description, and value set. The access attributes can be any of the following: read, write, update, etc. The description must indicate the format and size.

13.6.1 Processing Details of the Access Matrix Model

Figure 13.1 outlines the processing components of the access matrix system. A request to access an object will undergo the following steps:

- The user program or transaction makes a request to access a protectable object to the monitor.
- The monitor checks the user program (subject) identifier, and retrieves the access matrix row containing the object to which access is requested.

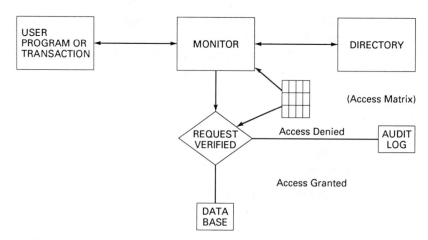

FIG. 13.1. Schematic of the components of the access matrix control system.

- The access matrix points to the relevant directory.
- The monitor gets the relevant information about the subject and object from the directory.
- The monitor verifies that the subject is authorized to access the requested object.
- A decision about the request is made by the monitor. If the request is denied, the monitor triggers an on-line terminal, which creates an audit trail or log. If the request is granted, then the monitor accesses the data base and returns the requested data item to the user program.

13.6.2 Processing Alternatives of the Access Matrix Model

The design of the monitor is very critical in cutting down on overhead during processing. The monitor should be flexible enough to incorporate some of the following processing alternatives:

- The monitor should be able to determine whether the class of subjects making a request is authorized to access the requested object. This would prevent it having to get the information from the access matrix or the directory.
- The monitor should be able to make determinations from either the access matrix or the directory, and not necessarily have to access both.
- The monitor should be able to go directly to the data base, bypassing the access matrix and directories, after a request is verified.
- The monitor should be able to update directories and put special emphasis on history (time) sensitive information.

13.7 THE RISK ASSESSMENT AS AN AID TO SELECTING A PROTECTION MECHANISM

Many organizations hesitate to initiate a security program because of their ignorance of the sensitivity of the data in their environment and the cost/benefit ratio in instituting security features.

This ignorance exists mainly due to the reluctance of the organization to conduct a risk assessment. Many of them prefer to institute security features only after a break in security occurs.

The purpose of performing a risk assessment is to obtain a quantitative statement of the potential problems to which the data processing facility is exposed, so that appropriate cost-effective security safeguards can be selected. It is assumed that, once armed with such information, no security measure will be selected that costs more than tolerating the problem will. The risk assessment should establish that threshold.

The risk analysis provides a rational approach toward choosing security safeguards. A security program should logically provide protection in the most economical manner. The following questions, therefore, should be answered in the course of a risk assessment:

- What are the specific results desired (that is, exactly how much security is required)?
- What is the proper balance between security program cost and the potential benefits?
- When trade-offs can be made between protection and recovery, and how much effort should be expended on each?

An important part of the security program involves determining what functions are performed or supported by the data base environment that is vital to the organization's survival. The advisability of providing security beyond this minimum can be determined largely through the cost/benefit analysis.

Freedom of information legislation may require organizations to allow their customers access to their records. How such requests would affect the current structure of the organization's data base can only be determined by a risk assessment.

Any risk assessment conducted at an early developmental stage of data design will be less costly and will allow more adequate security features to be built into developing systems at a lower cost than at a later stage, when systems are completed and may have to go through tremendous redesign phases and cost to implement similar and necessary security features.

The risk assessment conducted by corporations at an early stage of development need not be expensive. A useful set of baseline data can be obtained by conducting simple interviews and surveys in all departments and data processing groups.

13.8 RESOURCE ACCESS CONTROL FACILITY (RACF) AS A PROTECTION MECHANISM

RACF is a software product from IBM, which is designed to identify system users and control their access to protected resources.

RACF's authorization structure can be contrasted with a data set password mechanism. With typical password protection, a password is assigned to a specific data set. The system insures that the data set can be accessed only when that password is supplied.

Protected data sets can be accessed by anyone who knows the password. Obviously, there are control problems associated with restricting knowledge of the passwords.

There are also problems in withdrawing access to data sets. If three people know the password for a particular data set, and an administrator wants to take away one person's access rights, the password must be changed and the new password communicated to the users.

13.8.1 RACF Concepts

The RACF authorization structure is based on principles different from password protection. RACF eliminates the need for data set passwords.

With RACF, an administrator or auditor can tell which users are authorized to access which data sets. A user's right to access data set can be withdrawn simply by changing the structure.

The RACF authorization structure contains three kinds of elements: users, groups of users, and protected resources. It stores descriptions of users, groups, and resources in profiles contained in a special data set called the RACF data set. The types of resources that RACF protects are Direct Access Storage Device (DASD) data sets, tape volumes, DASD volumes, terminals, and applications.

Users, groups, and resources can be interrelated. A user can be a member of one or more groups. This membership allows the user to administer the group or to simply function within the group when accessing data. Both users and groups can be authorized to access protected resources. The type of access allowed corresponds to the different types of operations that can be performed in data handling.

RACF interfaces with the operating system in three main areas:

- Identification and verification of users.
- Authorization checking for access to protected resources.
- Monitoring to provide both immediate notification of security problems and a log for after-the-fact analysis

Once RACF has verified the user's identity, it builds a description of the user. This description is kept in memory for the duration of the job or on-line session.

Comparing this description with what the user can do is the basis for authority checking.

Authority checking is the basis for deciding whether a processing function or an access to RACF performs authority checking without any user or operator intervention. If the access is authorized, it is allowed; if unauthorized, it is denied.

RACF follows very specific rules for authority verification. First, it checks to see whether the user is authorized to the resource by inspecting the resource profile in the RACF data set. If this is not the case, then RACF uses its description of the protected resource. RACF determines whether the user is on the access list. If the user is, then RACF can decide whether the user should be authorized to perform the function requested.

If the user is not on the access list, RACF then checks to see whether the user's group is on the access list.

Monitoring or logging is used to record and subsequently report the occurrence of unauthorized access attempts. It also serves to provide evidence that the general security guidelines that have been implemented are being enforced. RACF uses two general types of monitoring: 1) logging if access to data or to the system occurs; and 2) logging if changes to the RACF profiles that define the authorization structures occur.

If an access attempt is unauthorized, it will not be permitted, or the profile change will not take place. Depending upon options set by administrators or by the resource owner, a log record will be written, and a message will be sent to a designated security console.

The log record contains the following:

- A normal time stamp.
- Identification of the user and group causing the action being logged.
- The reasons for logging.
- Levels of authority required and granted.
- Identification of the resource in question.
- Operands specified and the values specified for these operands when the RACF profiles are changed.

13.9 DEPARTMENT OF DEFENSE (DoD) SECURITY REQUIREMENTS

It should be noted that several of the protection mechanisms reported here are adequate for security in a commercial environment, but not in the military environment.

The Department of Defense requires a greater level of security than that required by commercial enterprises. Very often, vendors who wish to do business with the DoD are required to supply multilevel security according to the DoD Orange Book. For example, in multilevel security, it may often be found that the entire data base may be protected at one level, files within the data base at another level, and individual fields within the files at a third level.

The general consensus is that multilevel protection requires a large overhead in terms of the authorization tables that are required to maintain separate profiles for each level.

The protection mechanisms discussed in this chapter have proven, over the years, to be adequate for the wider audience. Vendors who want to do business with the DoD are very often advised as to the types of mechanisms that are acceptable to the DoD. The author does not intend to discuss multilevel security and the DoD Orange Book at any length. It is sufficient to say that suppliers to the DoD are well advised of the security requirements and those few who specialize in this level of security are prepared to provide adequate protection to the DoD. It would require too much to discuss that type of protection in a book of this type. The coverage of this will be left to more specialized publications.

13.10 SUMMARY

This chapter has served to discuss some of the advanced features of data base security, privacy, and integrity. It discussed the need for management's involvement and support of any effort in data security, a risk assessment to determine the sensitivity of the organization's data, and audit trails to determine who did what and when in terms of breaching the security.

In terms of protection mechanisms, two were discussed. The access matrix developed by the author, and the Resource Access Control Facility (RACF) developed by IBM. The chapter concluded by giving a detailed account of these protection mechanisms for the benefit of researchers interested in installing either of them in their organization.

The Orange Book published by the DoD was briefly mentioned. It is the author's opinion that, due to the specialized nature of multilevel protection mechanisms, and the overhead involved in running them, it is beyond the scope of this book to discuss them at greater length.

14

Disaster Recovery

14.1 INTRODUCTION

This chapter discusses an aspect of information resource management that is very often overlooked by the data processing industry. Disaster recovery is very seldom included as a concern when organizations discuss the planning for, managing, and controlling of the information resource.

This chapter deals with disaster recovery; the plans and procedures that should be in place in order to assist an organization in recovery from a disaster; the testing and execution of those plans and procedures; the personnel required to execute those plans; and the actions required during the disaster.

14.2 WHAT IS A DISASTER?

A disaster may be defined as a threat to which an organization is vulnerable. The threat may be classified as accidental or intentional. Disasters are sometimes classified as natural (acts of God) or manmade (perpetrated by man).

The categories of disasters that pose a threat to the organization's information resource, and the ones that will be discussed in this chapter are:

- Fire
- Flood
- Earthquakes
- Hostage situations

- Power loss
- Wind storms
- Snow or ice storms
- Equipment failure

14.3 WHAT IS A DISASTER RECOVERY PLAN?

A disaster recovery plan may be defined as a document that indicates what steps or actions will be taken by an organization if struck by a disaster, to declare a disaster, to continue processing information during the period of the disaster, and to render the information processing facility operable in a manner equivalent to that before the disaster occurred.

The disaster recovery plan sets forth the steps covering what actions will be taken in respect to:

- Personnel
- Equipment
- Supplies
- Suppliers
- Systems and programs
- Stored data

The next several sections discuss the various components of disaster recovery planning.

14.4 THE DISASTER RECOVERY TEAM

The overall function of the disaster recovery team is to undertake the various tasks that will allow an organization to continue its operational activities during a disaster and recover its operation once a disaster has been declared.

The composition, functions, and responsibilities of the recovery team are as shown in the following table:

Team Member	Title/Function
Team coordinator	Heads the team and chairs regular sessions of the team during a disaster.
Primary site restoration coordinator	Heads the group charged with the restoration of the primary site.
Recovery site coordinator	Heads the group charged with preparing the recovery site and processing at that site.
Disaster notification coordinator	Responsible for notifying all personnel of a disaster.

Management/administration coordinator	Responsible for reporting all management/administration decisions to the recovery team during a disaster and keeping management appraised of recovery efforts.
Application/user coordinator	Responsible for the group charged with the processing and maintenance of critical applications during a disaster and keeping users appraised of recovery efforts.
Systems software coordinator	Responsible for the group charged with the generation and maintenance of the operating system and all attendant software at the recovery site during a disaster.
Communications coordinator	Responsible for the group charged with the generation of control programs and maintenance of all communications equipment during a disaster.
Hardware/operations coordinator	Responsible for the group charged with operating all hardware at the recovery site, and production and distribution of reports and outputs to the organization during a disaster.
Command site coordinator	Responsible for selecting, equipping, and operating a site from which the recovery team will operate during a disaster.

The recovery team will use the following tools and output:

1. Tools used by recovery team:

   - Critical supplies list
   - Suppliers/salesmen list
   - Disaster notification list
   - List of items stored off-site
   - Equipment inventory list
   - List of critical programs

2. Output from the recovery team session:

   - The decision to process at recovery site or delay processing until restoration of primary site.
   - The level of service plan.
   - The security requirements list.
   - The schedule for running production jobs and the recovery site.
   - Transportation requirements.

14.5 REVIEW OF DATA CENTER OPERATIONS

The review of data center operations is the main data collection phase of the disaster recovery study. It allows the recovery team to determine the hardware/

software configuration of the center, and to examine what documents exist in the following areas:

Areas	Documents
Hardware configuration	Diagrams, layouts, or maps of the hardware and inventory lists.
Operating system environment	The operating system (e.g., MVS, DOS/VSE), including version or level numbers; TP monitors (CICS or VOLLIE), including version or level numbers; modems; controllers; and the number of terminals.
The number of operating hours and day of operations	Usage charts or diagrams showing hours the system is up per day and days per week. These documents are useful in selecting a backup site.
Operation of input-output areas	This includes documents showing distribution of reports. The recovery team should examine the I/O areas to evaluate the security of stored reports and printed sensitive information (e.g., payroll checks) and the retrieval of reports or printed information from holding bins.
Physical and data security	These include documented procedures for allowing access to the computer room. The recovery team should examine log-on procedures, authentication codes, and general protection mechanisms.
Scheduling of critical and noncritical jobs	The recovery team should examine existing scheduling documents to evaluate job mixes, run cycles, and priorities of major jobs.
Existing disaster recovery plans	The recovery team should examine all documents relating to disaster recovery and any recovery action plans.

14.6 REVIEW CURRENT BACK-UP AND RESTORE PROCEDURES

The purpose is to determine and evaluate how the organization currently backs up and restores its data files, teleprocessing monitors, and source libraries.

The recovery team will examine procedures in the following areas:

- Backup of CICS.
- Backup of VSAM files or other data bases.
- Backup of on-line and batch source libraries.

This phase will seek to determine what utilities are used to back up the above-listed items, how often the items are backed-up, and how many copies are kept on-site and sent off-site.

The recovery team will also evaluate the existing backup and restore procedures and make recommendations.

14.7 REVIEW CURRENT OFF-SITE
STORAGE PROCEDURES

The purpose of this phase is to examine and evaluate existing procedures at the organization's data center for transporting and storing backup copies of files at off-site locations.

The scope of the phase includes examining existing logs recording the identification of back-up files, the version of back-up, and the date of back-up.

The recovery team will examine the logs for signatures required to send files to the off-site storage and receipt of older versions of back-up files back at the data center.

The primary determination of this phase is how stored materials will be retrieved from the off-site location during a disaster. The recovery team will examine evidence that access (by phone) can be obtained to the off-site location during non-business hours and that particular versions or generations of back-up files can be easily obtained during the disaster.

The recovery team will also determine the security and authentication procedures in place to maintain the integrity of the organization's data at all times. It should be established that only authorized personnel can retrieve files, at all times, from the off-site location.

14.8 IDENTIFY AND RANK
CRITICAL APPLICATIONS

This is the most important phase of the study. It is from this phase that the recovery team obtains criteria that are useful in determining the adequacy of the recovery site.

During this phase, the team establishes the following:

- Data collection methods for all applications that will be processed during the disaster. The team determines cut-off times collecting this data and what other jobs are dependent on the successful collection of this data.
- The maximum allowable down-time during which the application can remain unprocessed without having a detrimental impact on the users.
- How source documents will be retained and used to re-generate files that may be destroyed for which there is no backup. For example, how will on-line data be recaptured if a disaster occurred between scheduled back-ups.
- The maximum level of service that will be acceptable to the users during the disaster and recovery periods. The team will determine what changes in processing frequency, number of on-line terminals, number of reports, and types of reports are acceptable.
- The priority of jobs and what jobs will be processed during the disaster.

- The minimum number of support staff, operators of terminals and printers, disk storage devices, and controllers that will be required to keep the applications going.

The recovery team will develop surveys to collect data that will allow for the identifying and ranking of the critical applications and services.

14.9 IDENTIFY CRITICAL SUPPLIERS

The purpose of this phase is to produce a comprehensive inventory of supplies and suppliers. The inventory will include:

- Identification of critical supplies and suppliers.
- Contacts within suppliers (including phone numbers during business and non-business hours).
- Departments responsible for the order and re-order of supplies.
- The location of temporary storage of supplies (partial amounts to keep a processing cycle going).
- Lead times for obtaining critical supplies.

The importance of this phase cannot be overemphasized. The ability to recover from a disaster and the time to recover is dependent on the availability of critical supplies.

The phase will also collect information on unique equipment that is critical to the recovery effort. This includes:

- Signature plates
- Microfiche or film readers
- MICR machines
- 96-column card readers

14.10 REVIEW THE BACK-UP SITE

During this phase, the recovery team will review the back-up site and determine whether the site can support the minimum requirements of the organization in the following areas:

- Operating system
- Data storage
- On-line and batch processing
- Physical and data security

The recovery team will seek to determine that the recovery site either has a native operating system (e.g., MVS, DOS/VSE) or can simulate (using VM) a compatible operating system for use by the data center during the disaster. The system (through its resident program) must be able to support any "fixes" that are required to run the critical programs of the center and allow for critical back-up and recovery of all data.

The recovery site must be able to support the data storage requirements of the data center. If storage media are not identical, then (through software) it must allow for that storage. For example, storage of data normally on 3350 disk on a 3380 disk, and vice versa.

The site must be able to support the minimum amount of terminals, controllers, and printers required by the center. The recovery team will ensure that all security requirements for physical and data security, report distribution and storage, and access to computer and work areas are met by the recovery site.

14.11 DEFINE THE SCOPE OF THE DISASTER RECOVERY STUDY

The purpose of this phase of the study is to set the scope of the disaster recovery action plan. The action plan is a step-by-step account of actions that must be taken by the organization's data center and user personnel to recover from a declared disaster.

The actions taken by the data center are determined to a large extent by the magnitude of destruction of the computing facilities.

The recovery team will interview recommended personnel at the data center to determine whether the plan should be written for total or partial destruction of the computer facilities.

The recovery team will deliver, at the end of the study, a comprehensive document detailing activities that must be undertaken at the center and in the affected departments to declare a disaster, notify all critical individuals, secure the damaged site after insurance assessment, move processing to the recovery site, and rebuild the damaged primary site.

14.12 DEVELOP INVENTORY PROCEDURES

This phase outlines procedures that the organization must adhere to in order to develop a comprehensive list of suppliers.

The output from this phase is used for two reasons: (1) insurance—to make a claim after a disaster, and (2) replacement—to determine what was lost or stolen and must be replaced.

The results of this phase will be a document showing what is available, who holds the item, how it can be ordered, and any substantive identifying information about the item.

14.13 DEVELOP
BACK-UP SITE CAPABILITIES

The purpose of this phase is to develop, test, and make available a back-up site at which the organization can process its data while the primary site is being restored following a disaster. The primary output from this phase will be a site compatible with the current site of the organization. The recovery team will undertake the following tasks during this phase:

- Generate a compatible operating system at the backup site. The operating system can be run in either a native mode (e.g., MVS, DOS/VSE) or be simulated using a VM-like operating system.
- Load all existing data for critical applications onto storage devices at the backup site. These include VSAM files, data bases, source libraries, load modules, and all required utilities.
- Test the ability to retrieve data, backup and restore the data, and support all requirements for printing and displaying that data.
- Generate a telecommunications system that will support the on-line processing requirements of the primary site. This will include NCP generation, loading and compiling of source programs for CICS, and any other TP monitors that are required. The recovery team will ensure that the required number of ports are available to support on-line terminals and that controllers and control programs are all tested and in working order.
- Compile, debug, and test critical applications that will be processed at the recovery site. The recovery team will ensure that all programs, including those with nonstandard "fixes" and "patches" can be processed at the recovery site.
- Run all core applications and make results available to the data center and users for comparison with results from the primary site.

The recovery team will turn over a complete documentation package for this phase of the project, including procedures for maintaining the software and applications at the recovery site to the enterprise executives.

14.14 DEVELOPMENT AND TEST
OF A RECOVERY PLAN

The purpose of this phase is to develop and test a comprehensive disaster recovery action plan. The action plan is a step-by-step account of actions that must be taken by the organizations data center staff and user personnel to process data during a disaster and restore the primary site.

The action plan will include information on the following topics:

- Activities by user departments

- Disaster notification list
- Disaster recovery activities
- Vital areas of recovery
- Telecommunications requirements
- Primary and recovery sites' security
- Plan testing and maintenance
- Alternate processing approaches

During this phase, the organization's data center and user departments will be broken down into various activity areas for the purpose of effecting the disaster recovery plan and meeting the stated objectives of the plan.

The activity areas are better defined as areas in which certain disaster recovery related activities are conducted to effect recovery of the primary site and data processing at the recovery site. For example, the data center may be broken down into the following activity areas:

- Management/administration
- Systems programming
- Applications programming
- Production scheduling and operations
- User department services
- Equipment manufacturer services
- Transportation
- Recovery team services
- Data processing steering committee

The activities of the management/administration activity area includes:

- Coordination of restoration effort at the primary site.
- Coordination of the retrieval of vital items from various off-site storage locations and delivery to the recovery site.
- Scheduling of the production of jobs based on priorities established when critical applications were identified and ranked.
- Monitoring of the backup and recovery procedures during the disaster period.
- Monitoring of the service levels during the disaster period.

The recovery team should develop a list of personnel who should be notified when a disaster occurs. The list will include persons within and outside the organization. Those persons outside the organization will include the police, fire department, equipment suppliers, and insurance representatives.

The comprehensive action plan will include activities that must be carried out at the primary and recovery sites during the disaster period.

The activities at the primary site will include:

- Disaster declaration.
- Disaster notification.

- Damage assessment by the insurance agent.
- Vital items retrieval.
- Site clean up.
- Physical security maintenance.
- Repair/replace equipment and computer room.
- Load and test operating system and applications programs.
- Back-up of vital items.
- Back-up and restoration of input transactions.
- Replace missing documentation and procedure manuals.

The recovery team must identify items and vital areas within the organization that must be recovered and placed in a ready status to effect the disaster recovery action plan. During this phase, the team will identify vital functions, procedures, and reports that must be preserved in each user department to assist in the recovery.

The recovery team will determine the telecommunications needs of the organization during this phase. The requirements will not be limited to the number of modems or controllers that will be required to keep the data center functional, but will examine modifications that may be required. These modifications may include:

- Modifying VTAM books to define the terminals and printers at the recovery site.
- Modifying VTAM books for remote terminals to incorporate various macros used by NCP.
- Cataloging VTAM books in the source statement library.
- Includeing VTAM books in start-up books for VTAM.
- LINK—editing the assembled NCP statements.

The recovery team will evaluate and document, in the action plan, the security requirements at the primary and recovery sites. The evaluation should not be limited to physical security, but should also include data security considerations.

In the area of data security, the recovery team should evaluate the threats to which the data center is exposed and the existing protection mechanisms in place to counter those threats. The team will determine the adequacy of existing protection mechanisms and recommend further protection if the situation warrants it.

14.14.1 Test of the Disaster Recovery Action Plan

The recovery team should conduct tests of the disaster recovery action plan to ensure that:

- The plan is complete and workable.
- The materials and data are available and usable to perform alternate processing for critical applications.

- The system and library files and application software and current and processable.
- Processing can be resumed as planned.

The plan should be tested at three levels:

Level 1—Adequacy of off-site storage of files and documentation.
Level 2—Capability to restore the primary site using off-site files and documentation.
Level 3—Capability of producing a comparable operating system and processing environment at the recovery site.

The areas to be tested will include:

- Backup for:
    VSAM files
    Data bases
    JCL
    Operating System

- Documentation back-up for:
    Operations
    Operating System
    Applications
    User Procedures

- Supplies back-up for:
    Special forms
    Pre-printed forms
    Input documents

The recovery team should assist the organizations data center in conducting simulated disasters and "fire drill" tests. These tests may be as simple as bringing down the entire computer system, without prior notice, and restoring it from tapes and files stored off-site to full-scale tests with all areas, including user departments, involved.

The team will develop procedures to enable the data center to keep the action plan current; make additions, deletions, or revisions as the situation warrants; and monitor the performance of the plan in areas, such as:

- The ability to generate a compatible system at the primary site from stored off-site data.
- The ability to retrieve items from off-site locations.
- The ability to run on-line and batch programs at the recovery site.
- The ability to update hardware and software at recovery site.
- The ability to back-up the activities of critical personnel.

  ▪ The ability to evaluate required security features at both the recovery and primary sites.

14.15 DATA COLLECTION FOR A DISASTER RECOVERY PLAN

The data that constitutes the disaster recovery plan is collected, primarily through surveys, from all functional areas of the organization. The surveys are constructed so as to obtain information on the organization's business functions, critical personnel, supplies, potential loss due to a disaster, ability to remain functioning during and after a disaster, and technology requirements.

Exhibits B and C illustrate two questionnaires developed to collect business function and data processing information.

Exhibit B.
Questionnaire to Determine Business Functions
(Disaster Recovery Action Plan)

Question 1. List the business functions that are critical to the operation of your department.

Question 2. List the functions in your department that are related to the processing of computerized data.

Question 3. List all employees who perform critical functions in your department and are vital to the corporation's disaster recovery effort.

Question 4. List all supplies (both computer and non-computer) that are critical to the operation of your department.

Question 5. In the event of a disaster, what functions must be performed in order for the department to survive and recover?

Question 6. List all vital items in your department that should be stored off-site.

Question 7. In the event of a disaster, what activities must be conducted in your department that will allow MIS to recover the primary site?

Question 8. In the event of a disaster, what activities must be conducted in your department that will allow MIS to process data at the recovery site?

Question 9. What are the transportation needs for the relocation of personnel, movement of data and reports, and conveyance of vital documents during a disaster?

Question 10. What level of protection and security will be required for your transportation needs during a disaster?

Question 11. List all critical reports that must be produced by MIS for your department during a disaster.

Question 12. List all personnel within and outside of your department who should be notified about a disaster.

Question 13. List all personnel critical to your department's survival, to whom a copy of the disaster recovery plan should be given.

Question 14. List, in order of priority, all critical reports that must be produced by MIS in order for your department to survive a disaster.

Question 15. Indicate off-site storage of all vital items and how they can be retrieved during a disaster.

Question 16. In the event of a disaster, what is the minimum number of terminals that must be located at the recovery site to support your department?

Question 17. Who are the critical people who will be required to operate these terminals?

Question 18. In the event of a disaster, how would you capture and record data that is now entered on-line into the computer system?

Question 19. If the on-line system is down for several days, would MIS have to produce any special reports for you that they are not now providing?

Question 20. Are you now contracted to produced any reports for other departments or parties by specific dates and times?

Question 21. Are there any legal filings of specific reports to federal or other government agencies that must be adhered to during a disaster?

Question 22. Indicate the monetary loss to your department if you could not process data for:

(a) 10—20 hours
(b) 1—2 days
(c) 3—5 days
(d) 6—10 days

Exhibit C.
Questionnaire to Determine DP Needs
(Disaster Recovery Action Plan)

Question 1. List all equipment (including model numbers) at the primary site.

Question 2. List all suppliers (including salesman/number) for the primary site.

Question 3. List the location of off-site storage and how items can be retrieved during an emergency.

Question 4. List the procedures to be followed to declare a disaster and move to an off-site facility.

Question 5. List the procedures to be followed to declare a disaster and restore the primary site.

Question 6. Indicate how physical security will be maintained during a disaster.

Question 7. Indicate what operating system and program testing will be done after recovery of the primary site.

Question 8. List all vital items that will be required to recover the primary site (assuming a total shutdown).

Question 9. List all critical personnel required to recover the primary site.

Question 10. List any unique requirements for any equipment at the primary site.

Question 11. Indicate how the back-up of vital items will be done during the disaster.

Question 12. List all personnel who will be notified of a disaster at the primary site.

Question 13. Indicate how items not backed-up will be reconstructed and added to the input for the primary site recovery.

14.16 A SYNOPSIS OF DISASTER RECOVERY ACTIVITIES

There is a cycle of activities that an organization must go through to declare and recover from a disaster. That cycle was discussed in detail in this chapter. In summary, those activities are as follows:

- The recovery team is to report to the command center
- The coordinator notifies the insurance adjustor
- The notification coordinator notifies all personnel of the disaster
- The insurance adjustor examines site
- The recovery team examines site
- The Manufacturers' representatives examines site
- The Representative presents an outage report to the recovery team
- The recovery team makes an inventory of items
- The recovery team decides to remain at the primary site or process at the recovery site
- The recovery team notifies company executives of recovery of disaster
- The recovery team orders vital supplies
- The recovery team retrieves vital items from off-site storage
- The recovery team prepares the recovery site
- The recovery team coordinates movement of staff to the recovery site
- The recovery team notifies staff of alternate duties
- The recovery team suspends all applications development and maintenance
- The recovery team moves needed supplies to the recover site
- The recovery team loads operating system at the recovery site
- The recovery team loads production programs and data files
- The recovery team hooks up terminals
- The recovery team runs scheduled production jobs at the recovery site

14.17 SUMMARY

This chapter discussed all aspects of disaster recovery in some detail. The various phases of a disaster recovery plan were highlighted, although in no particular order.

The output of the study that forms the basis of this chapter is a complete action plan. The action plan is now being marketed by AKI Group, Inc. In addition, the same organization is offering a three-day course on disaster recovery at various locations throughout the United States and Canada.

Bibliography

Atre, S. *Data Base: Structured Techniques for Design, Performance, and Management.* New York: John Wiley & Sons, 1988.

Brathwaite, K. S. *Analysis, Design, and Implementation of Data Dictionaries.* New York: McGraw-Hill, 1988.

Brathwaite, K. S. *Data Administration.* New York: John Wiley & Sons, 1985.

Brathwaite, K. S. *An Implementation of a Data Dictionary to Support Databases Designed Using the Entity-Relationship (E-R) Approach.* New York: North-Holland Publishing, ER Institute, 1983.

Brathwaite, K. S. Management involvement in data security, integrity, and privacy. *AGT Tech. Memo,* no. 15, 1980.

Brathwaite, K. S. A study of data base security, integrity and privacy in a large public utility. *AGT Tech. Memo,* no. 20, 1980.

Brathwaite, K. S. *Systems Design in DB Environment.* New York: McGraw-Hill, 1989.

Brown, D. RACF—A program to enhance security and control. *EDPACS,* vol. 6, no. 12, Institute of Internal Auditors, June 1979.

Brown, P. S. Computer security—A survey. *NCC,* AFIPS Press, 1976.

Brown, P. S. *Security: Checklist for Computer Center Self-Audits.* Washington D.C.: AFIPS Press, 1979.

Canning, R. G., A new view of data dictionaries. *EDP Analyzer,* July, 1981.

Chen, P. P., ed. *Proceedings of the International Conference on Entity-Relationship Approach to Systems Analysis and Design.* New York: North-Holland Publishing, 1979.

Chen, P. P., ed. *Proceedings of the International Conference on Entity-Relationship Approach to Information Modelling and Analysis.* New York: North-Holland Publishing, 1981.

Courtney, R. H. Security risk assessment in electronic data processing systems. *AFIPS Conf. Proc. 46,* 1979, NCC 97–104. Washington D. C.: AFIPS Press, 1977.

Davenport, R. A. Data analysis for database design. *The Australian Computer Journal,* vol. 10, no. 4. 1979, pp. 122–137.

Dinardo, C. T. *Computers and Security.* Washington, D.C.: AFIPS Press, 1978.

Durell, W. Disorder to discipline via the data dictionary. J. *Systems Management,* May 1983.

Durell, W. R. *Data Administration.* New York: McGraw-Hill, 1985.

Engelman, C. "Audit and Surveillance of Multi-level Computing Systems," MTR-3207. The Mitre Corporation, June 1975.

Fernandez, E. B. *Database Security and Integrity.* New York: Addison-Wesley, 1981.

Fosdick, H. *Using IBM's ISPF Dialog Manager.* New York: Van Nostrand Reinhold, 1987.

Gillenson, M. *Database: Step-by-step.* New York: John Wiley & Sons, 1985.

Gillenson, M. and Goldberg, R. *Strategic Planning Systems Analysis and Data Base Design.* New York: John Wiley & Sons, 1984.

Hoffman, L. J. "The Formulary Model for Access Control and Privacy in Computer Systems," SCAC Report No. 119. May 1970.

Hsiao, D. K. *Computer Security.* San Diego, CA: Academic Press, Inc., 1979.

Hubbard, G. *Computer-Assisted Data Base Design.* New York: Van Nostrand Reinhold, 1981.

Kahn, B. K. A method for describing the information required by the data base design process. *Proc. Int. ACM/Sigmod Conf. Management of Data,* 1976.

Katzan, H. *Computer Data Security.* New York: Van Nostrand Reinhold, 1973.

Korth, H. F. and Silbersehatz, R. *Database System Concepts.* New York: McGraw-Hill, 1986.

Larson, B. *The Database Experts Guide to DB2.* New York: McGraw-Hill, 1988.

Leong-Hong, B. W. and Plagman, B. K. *Data Dictionary/Directory Systems: Administration, Implementation, and Usage.* New York: John Wiley & Sons, 1982.

Lusardi, F. *The Database Experts Guide to SQL.* New York: McGraw-Hill, 1988.

Lusk, E. L. A practical design methodology for the implementation of IMS databases using the E-R model. *ACM,* vol. 4, 1980. pp. 9–21.

Martin, J. and McClure, C. *Structured Techniques: The Basis for CASE.* Englewood Cliffs, NJ: Prentice-Hall, 1988.

Novak, D. and Fry, J. The state of the art of logical database design. *Proc. 5th Texas Conf. Computing Systems (IEEE),* Long Beach, CA, 1976.

Statland, N. Data security and its impact on EDP auditing. *EDPACS,* vol. 3., no. 4, Institute of Internal Auditors, Oct. 1979.

Weldon, J. L. *Database Administration.* New York: Plenum Press, 1981.

Whitmore, J. C. "Design for Multics Security Enhancements." ESD-TR-74-176, Honeywell Info. Systems, 1974.

Yao, S. B. An integrated approach to logical database design. *NYU Symposium on Database Design,* May 18–19, 1978.

Index